THE KEYS

TO THE

UNIVERSE

THE KEYS

TO THE

UNIVERSE

Access the ancient secrets by attuning to
the power and wisdom of the cosmos

DIANA COOPER
& KATHY CROSSWELL

FINDHORN PRESS

ISBN 978-1-84409-500-1

Edited by Sabine Weeke and Carol Shaw
Proofread by Michael Hawkins
Cover, interior design by Damian Keenan
Printed and bound in the European Union

3 4 5 6 7 8 9 10 16 15 14 13 12 11

Published by
Findhorn Press
117-121 High Street,
Forres IV36 1AB,
Scotland, UK

t +44 (0)1309 690582
f +44 (0)131 777 2711
e info@findhornpress.com
www.findhornpress.com

Contents

The Portals

The Kingdoms

Contents

DEDICATION

*I dedicate this book with much love
to my granddaughters Kailani and Maya.*
Diana

*I dedicate this book with my heartfelt thanks
and love to my dearest family and friends
who have graced me with pure unconditional love,
during the most challenging time in my life.*
Kathy

Introduction

When I had finished my latest book *2012 and Beyond*, I was looking forward to a little rest before starting any other project. But then the inevitable happened: I spent time with my friend Kathy Crosswell, who co-authored *Enlightenment Through Orbs* and *Ascension Through Orbs* with me. As we chatted my guide Kumeka came in. He told us that the spiritual realms wanted us to write a very important book. We would have to do it together as it was to be a very high-frequency piece of work to help move many people on the planet forward. He added that neither of us could create it on our own, only our combined energy would take us to the level we needed to reach in order to bring the special information through in a pure way.

He then informed us that the book was to be called *The Keys to the Universe*. We were overawed. It seemed almost a presumption to write anything of such a magnitude. Looking at each other in total silence for a while we contemplated the huge responsibility this inferred.

Kumeka would give us no information except that we must start in the New Year of 2010, but not before. When I phoned Thierry Bogliolo, my publisher at Findhorn Press, he loved the title and asked for some information for the back cover of the book to give to the distributors. I told him I would try to find out what the book was about! Kathy and I asked Kumeka for information for the back cover and he told us what to write. We knew no more than that! There cannot be many publishers who trust so much that they will be prepared to publish a book without knowing anything other than the title and the blurb on the back cover. Thierry Bogliolo and his spiritual publishing house, Findhorn Press, are very special though. They make all their decisions on a fifth-dimensional basis.

This book still seemed a daunting task but we consoled ourselves that the Illumined Ones would not have chosen us to do it if we were not ready.

The next time Kathy and I met something even more awesome and unexpected happened. We were channelling together when suddenly the energy in the room went totally still, the lights dimmed. We knew someone carrying a higher frequency than we had ever experienced was trying to contact us. It was like the first time a Seraphim came in but much more profound and powerful. We looked at each other questioning, 'Who is it?' then relaxed more deeply and waited. It was Source! He/She wanted to connect with us personally to tell us how important *The Keys to the Universe* was. Source also gave us both personal messages, mostly about looking after ourselves correctly with diet, exercise, meditation and fun. We were both told to give our children and members of our family quality one-to-one time. Kathy was advised to connect with the wisdom of the indigenous people and I was asked to go on holiday to the Arctic, which I did. I cannot put in words how we felt after this experience: overwhelmed, elated, incredulous, unbelieving and totally nurtured – our feelings were all intermingled. I guess, the predominant feelings were a sense of disbelief, rapture and wonder.

God came to touch Kathy again as we began working on the book. In January 2010, on a very cold snowy day Kathy and I sat down to connect with our guides in order to receive information for *The Keys to the Universe*.

Immediately Kathy said, 'Oh, just a minute.' She fell silent and very still, with her eyes closed. A few moments later she opened them and told me, 'I was transported to a golden globe of Christ light in the universe. God was sitting there. He said, 'Take this,' and handed me the purest drop of water. He said that we are to give it to others through the book. I took it and looked up to thank him, and he had gone.'

Water symbolizes the life force of the planet and all on it, it is infused with God and the Christ Light. It is pure, innocent, life giving, cleansing and carries cosmic love, so it is the glue to the universe. It conducts electricity, sound and vibrations. Once again we felt quite overwhelmed with the importance of our task.

When we wrote the Orbs books many Archangels and three Seraphim came to connect with us, which they said was because they wanted to experience our energy. For the *Keys to the Universe*, my guide Kumeka and Kathy's guide Wywyvsil were our main informants, with Metatron overseeing the project. On one occasion Kumeka could not get us to understand the concept he was explaining and he suddenly stepped aside and allowed Seraphina, a Seraphim we had a connection with before, to come in and impress the information onto us. Then she withdrew and Kumeka returned and continued.

We were told that some of you will find certain Keys more relevant to you than others and will focus on those – this is perfectly all right. Others will want to tune into all of them to become cosmic masters, the more people that do this the better.

As we received the information for the book I was aware of how well prepared I had been by my previous books, especially by *A Little Light on the Spiritual Laws, New Light on Ascension, The Wonder of Unicorns* and *Discover Atlantis*. These provided foundations for my comprehension of the wisdom imparted to us now. The amount and depth of knowledge that Kathy and I received for *Enlightenment Through Orbs* and *Ascension Through Orbs* was also essential. However, we trust that we are passing the information in *The Keys to the Universe* on in a form that everyone can readily understand and act upon.

When we were writing the *Orbs* books we were told that Lakuma was the ascended aspect of Sirius. Now though we have been informed that its true name is Lakumay. Two years ago, when the other books were written, people were only ready to access the energy of Lakuma. With the additional 'y' to make it Lakumay faster frequency, angel energy is available and the general consciousness is now ready to accept this vibration. It is another reminder that everyone is moving forward very quickly.

I perceive the whole universe differently after writing this book. The Keys that excited me most were those held in the bird kingdom, time and speed, sacred geometry and sonic sounds but I find it quite difficult just to choose a few. As I reread the script I find more information or exercises that trigger a deep response within me. Kathy said, 'What excited me most about this book was how we were guided to always hold it in the highest energy, with only positive intentions clearly for the greatest good for all. I love working with my spiritual guides for they make me know how loved and lucky I am. I am so grateful to them.'

Now I am creating a restful summer so that I can practise the exercises and meditations that Kumeka gave me for this project!

Please read this book and activate the Keys so that you, the whole world and this universe will benefit. The Keys are that important!

The 50 Keys
to the Universe –
An Overview

We have been given 50 Keys to the universe: the two Golden Cosmic Keys held in Hollow Earth and Sirius, and 48 further Keys held by the ancient civilizations and cultures, the portals, the kingdoms and universal aspects and concepts. Each Key accesses part of the knowledge of the universe, for example how to use the energy of the sun, the wisdom of the trees, the messages of animals, an understanding of the properties of water or how to connect to angels.

We give specific information about each Key, the wisdom it holds and how to access it energetically. By working with the visualisations, exercises and sounds you will be able to attune to those Keys you are ready to work with. We suggest that, after reading about a Key, you listen to the sound on the accompanying CD.

You may be drawn to one of the Keys in particular or to several of them, and we suggest you focus on these until you understand and can access the wisdom they hold. On the other hand, you may find that they all resonate and you want to attune to them all. In that case you may want to start at the beginning and work steadily through all the exercises, expanding and growing as you do so. Or you may want to choose whichever ones appeal to you at a given time. Do whatever feels right to you. And remember that when you listen to the orchestrated sections of the CD for Hollow Earth or Sirius you receive all the energy of their Keys. Magic can occur.

When you understand and can access the wisdom of one of the 48 Keys you expand your consciousness. When you hold all the Keys to the universe you are an enlightened ascended master and you can access the true blueprint of Earth and help to bring it back.

~ *The First Golden Cosmic Key - Hollow Earth* ~

HOLLOW EARTH is the divine blueprint for the planet. It holds the plan for all of the ANCIENT CIVILIZATIONS and each one of these contain part of the universal wisdom. Each aspect of cosmic energy is known as a Key.

1. Atlantis
2. Lemuria
3. Mu
4. Petranium - the ancient civilization that seeded Africa and the African races
5. Angala - the birthing of Earth

The ANCIENT CULTURES all hold Keys to the universe, one to the wisdom of Lemuria and twelve to that of Atlantis.

6. The Aborigines who grounded the energy of Lemuria.

The twelve tribes holding the energy of Atlantis:

7. The Incas of South America, led by Thoth
8. The Aztecs of South America, led by Isis
9. The Babylonians, led by Horus
10. The Egyptians, led by Ra
11. The Innuit, led by Sett
12. The Native Americans, led by Imhotep
13. The Kahunas of Hawaii, led by Hermes
14. The Tibetans, led by Zeus
15. The Mayans of South America, led by Aphrodite
16. The Mesopotamians, led by Apollo
17. The Greek culture, led by Poseidon
18. The Maoris of New Zealand, led by Hera

To reach the stars, the angelic realms and the seventh dimension you either go through your Stellar Gateway chakra into the cosmos – or you go through your Earth Star into Hollow Earth. Preferably both.

There are twelve entry/exit points between Hollow Earth and surface Earth and into the cosmos, which act as PORTALS and also hold Keys:

19. The Pyramids, Egypt, are connected to Sirius
20. Mount Shasta, California, is linked to the Pleiades
21. The Mayan Pyramid of Guatemala, is connected to Venus
22. Agata, Northern Russia, is linked to the Pleiades
23. The pyramid under the Panthenon in Greece is connected to Orion
24. The pyramid in the mountains of Tibet is linked to the spiritual aspect of Sirius
25. The Pyramid under Machu Picchu, Peru, is connected to Saturn and the Moon
26. The Hollow Earth cosmic portal in North and South Dakota, Nebraska, Kansas and Oklahoma is linked to Source via the Pleiades
27. Honolulu is connected to Venus
28. The Dogon Portal, Mali, Africa is linked to Sirius
29. The Bermuda Triangle is connected to Neptune
30. The ocean near Fiji is linked to Alcyon, the Pleiades

In addition many KINGDOMS can be accessed through Hollow Earth and each of these hold a Key to the universe:

31. The bird kingdom
32. The animal kingdom
33. The kingdom of the ocean beings
34. The elemental kingdom
35. The angelic kingdom
36. The deva kingdom, including reptiles

~ The Second Golden Cosmic Key – Sirius ~

SIRIUS is one of the four ascension stars, planets and constellations connected with Earth. It holds information about spiritual technology, sacred geometry, science and higher mental understandings. Those souls who wish to bring these particular aspects forward on Earth will train in Sirius before incarnation. These universal aspects can be accessed through the Golden Cosmic Key of Sirius and they each hold a Key to the energies of the universe:

37. Time (and speed)
38. Other dimensions – Ascended Masters, Higher Self, Monad
39. Other planets, stars and galaxies
40. The nature kingdom – the elements

41. Sacred geometry
42. Light, containing spiritual information
43. Sonic sounds (dolphins)
44. Golden Earth (qualities of Golden Atlantis and 2032)
45. The cosmic heart
46. Pure love (divine connection)
47. Spiritual laws (alchemy and magic)
48. Oneness (the qualities – telepathy, communication)

PART I

Hollow Earth

Hollow Earth is the seventh-dimensional divine blueprint for the planet. It contains the design for all of the ancient civilizations and each one of these holds a Key to the universal energies.

Hollow Earth is an energetic space or cosmic chakra, right in the centre of our planet.

Within this chakra is held all the ancient knowledge of our Earth, including why this planet was brought into being by Source in the first place. It holds one of the two Golden Cosmic Keys to the Universe.

Many spiritual beings 'reside' in Hollow Earth. All are ethereal and seventh-dimensional, living in total harmony. For example, representatives of all the wise ancient cultures hold the living memory of their knowledge and wisdom within this place. These are ancient Atlanteans, Lemurians, beings from Mu and from Petranium, the original settlers in Africa, as well as from the time of Angala, which was the time of Earth's birth.

The more recent indigenous peoples have a lineage back to Atlantis – the Incas and Aztecs of South America, the Babylonians, the Egyptians, the Innuit, the Native Americans, the Kahunas of Hawaii, the Tibetans, the Mesopotamians, the Greek, the Mayans and the Maoris – and you can access their ancient wisdom through Hollow Earth. All of these tribes hold Keys.

The Lemurian lineage is the Aborigine culture, which holds a cosmic Key. Ancient Maori, Polynesian, tribal African and ancient Hawaian cultures also link back to Lemuria but it is their later Atlantean wisdom that holds the Key.

The ancient African lineage is Petranium.

Representatives of the spirits of all animals and birds also hold energy here, as do those of the elemental and nature kingdoms. Every species of animal, bird, tree, flower, fungus or elemental is found here whether or not it is extinct on the surface. For example, dodos, the flightless birds no longer on Earth reside here too. There is also a portal that leads to the dragon kingdom where dragon wisdom is found.

Hollow Earth is a seventh-dimensional paradise.

~ Portals ~

Portals are special places where the energy is higher and where we (and the angels) can access teachings, energies and light. Once in a portal you can easily be transported into higher energies for transformation. There are also beings who can access Earth directly, without using a portal, like the Pleiadeans who come to Earth to radiate healing to us.

Light containing spiritual information and knowledge radiates from certain stars and planets through twelve portals into Hollow Earth. Here it alters the blueprint of Earth in the highest possible way. Then Lady Gaia takes the amended blueprint and spreads its higher energy throughout the planet. This has an affect on us all.

The twelve portals that act as entry points on Earth for light from the stars are:

- The Great Pyramid, Egypt, which connects to Sirius;
- Mount Shasta, California, which links to the Pleiades;
- The Mayan Pyramid of Guatemala, which links to Venus;
- Agata, Northern Russia, which links to the Pleiades;
- The pyramid under the Panthenon in Greece, which links to Orion;
- The pyramid in the mountains of Tibet, which links to Lakumay, the spiritual aspect of Sirius;
- The pyramid under Machu Picchu, Peru, which links to Saturn and the Moon;
- The Hollow Earth cosmic portal in North and South Dakota, Nebraska, Oklahoma and Kansas, which links to Source via the Pleiades;
- Honolulu, which links to Venus;
- The Dogon Portal, Mali, Africa, which links to Lakumay, Sirius;
- The Bermuda Triangle, which links to Neptune;
- The ocean near Fiji, which links to Alcyon, the Pleiades.

~ *The Pyramid of Hollow Earth* ~

When you are in the central point of Hollow Earth you can access all the energies that are available through the portals. Anchored here is a pyramid of light with a crystal on top of it that turns constantly, radiating the wisdom and knowledge of the ancient civilizations and thirteen cultures as well as the stars and planets to which they are connected.

As above so below – the Great Pyramid of Hollow Earth was mirrored in Atlantis by the pyramids of the protective Dome over that continent. Information from all the stars is drawn into the pyramid and individual data can be accessed via the correct frequency. If you are focussed on Egypt, for example, and telepathically connect with the right vibration in the pyramid, you can draw out threads of Egyptian wisdom.

Each of the twelve portals holds a Key to Hollow Earth. The Keys are the notes of the ascension planets, stars and galaxies. When we hear them all together, we are in touch with the fifth-dimensional blueprint for Earth.

- Neptune   G
- Sirius   A
- Orion   D
- The Pleiades   C
- Earth   B

Venus, Saturn and the Moon are not ascension planets, so their notes are not relevant here.

~ *Two-way interdimensional portals* ~

Tibet; Stonehenge, UK; Machu Picchu, Peru and the Great Zimbabwe in Africa house the four two-way interdimensional portals on Earth. Two of these, Tibet and Machu Picchu are entrances to Hollow Earth.

Through these four special portals angels and other seventh-dimensional beings can go out into the cosmos as well as enter the planet. The mighty ones congregate at these portals and the land here is full of Source light.

~ *The Great Crystal of Hollow Earth* ~

The Great Crystal of Hollow Earth contains all knowledge of Earth and its place in the Universe. It receives energy directly from Source through the four ascension planets, stars and constellations, Neptune, Orion, Sirius and the Pleiades.

People can access this great Crystal when they open their twelve chakras and connect their roots down through the cosmic portal of Hollow Earth, which is located in the United States.

~ *The Universal Angel Gersisa* ~

The Universal Angel Gersisa has her retreat in Hollow Earth and breathes life force into this chakra and into Lady Gaia. And Lady Gaia's energy fills Hollow Earth and encompasses the whole planet.

Hollow Earth is pure light. The Universal Angel Gersisa is grey and this is a merging of the masculine energy white and the feminine energy black. She radiates light down the ley lines helping to keep the whole planet informed and steady. When Gersisa is filmed as an Orb, she appears as grey and white, radiating like a fan from a central point. This is because she is still connected to the ley lines wherever she is, which shows as her grey energy while she continues to send out fingers of pure white. See the Orb of Universal Angel Gersisa below.

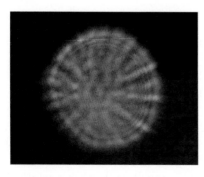

The Universal Angel Gersisa.
She appears as grey Orb and sends pure
white light down the leylines.

Photograph by Marie Daly

~ *Sun and moon* ~

On the surface of the planet we have a sun and moon, providing dark and light, day and night. In Hollow Earth, they have their own separate divine masculine and feminine energy sources, but, unlike our sun and moon, they both radiate at the same time. There is no day and night.

~ *What does Hollow Earth do for the planet?* ~

Hollow Earth holds the energy of Source at the seventh dimension within the planet. It is the blueprint for Earth. Here it is peaceful, pure, loving, calm, yet powerful and happy. All knowledge is known and understood – how to use moon energy, how plants thrive and our symbiotic relationship with animals. The indigenous people accessed the knowledge, and brought it to the surface to live it. It is time to connect with the true blueprint of Earth once more and bring it back again. The Keys to the Universe enable you to do so.

The surface of Earth should be a mirror of the centre. All aspects of nature, which is seventh-dimensional in the middle of the Earth, can be the same on the surface. We can access it through our roots, through the Earth Star. We have always been told: 'As above so below'. This is what we are aiming for.

Everything we need to know can be found in Hollow Earth but few can touch its pure, precious light without abusing it. It is so important and powerful that we must prepare ourselves for the possibility.

~ *Bringing the world into harmony* ~

To heal the world we need to find the sound of each continent separately and then bring them all together in harmony. The harmonization is the key, which will dissolve plugs or caps across the Earth and bring 2032 forward.

Whenever I have had the opportunity during recent seminars I have divided the attendees into groups to represent the different continents. Each section creates a song, chant or tone to reflect the energy of the part of the world they have chosen. Then all come together to contribute their sound in a way that brings everyone into harmony. Invariably by the end we can recognize that each group is different and at the same time there is a great feeling of oneness.

Kathy and I thought it would be so much more potent if we had the notes for each continent. When we asked Kumeka he said that he would have to take instruction from the Intergalactic Council before he could give us this information as it was incredibly powerful and must be used with wisdom and care. A few days later he said he had been given permission and so here are the notes!

- Arctic   A
- Antarctic   G
- Asia   D
- America   F
- South America   C
- Africa   B
- Europe   E
- Australasia   E

~ What Archangel Sandalphon said to Kathy about Hollow Earth ~

Twice the energy of Hollow Earth has been entrusted to those who are enlightened. The energy is the purest you will find. It encompasses everything people hold so close yet take for granted, such as the first cry of a baby, warm wind on your face, the taste of purest water, the sound of air, the pure song of a bird, the kindness yet firmness of Earth under your feet. It is so precious yet we entrust this life force to you. We trust you to breathe with it, to be of it, to understand how delicate and perfect, powerful and amazing this energy is.

There are many on the surface who will never and must never touch and feel this energy. They will not understand it and could snuff it out in an instant. Many people will feel it but never understand it. There are some who have the vision and memory, sound and vibration to breathe with Hollow Earth. They can move through Hollow Earth and out to the planets and beyond. It is these people who will transform the surface into a gentle, calm, tranquil, warm, loving place.

As you look at people around you they have mixed energies. Those who are the same on the inside as on the outside are the ones who will access Hollow Earth. It is my role to act as gatekeeper and encourage everyone to look within themselves to become a true, pure custodian of the life force of the planet and I will not let anyone pass until their intention and their energetic memory, is aligned and ready for use for the greater good of all.

Many people will never access the wonder of Hollow Earth. They cannot do it yet. A smile or laughter is infectious and those that do access it will bring the magic to life for those who do not. Others will get caught in the happiness, glow and wonder of the universe and this will gradually enlighten people. They will not be able to help themselves. They will become happy.

Source is entrusting you with the heartbeat of the planet. An analogy would be of a baby in the womb, waiting, full of knowledge and promise to give you. Be the best parents you can be. When your access into the energy of Hollow Earth has been accepted it is the time to fully ignite the Stellar Gateway. It is at this point that all that has been and will be, will come together. You become a person who is humble, grateful and very capable. You will have the wisdom of what knowledge and direction to share and when to spread it.

Then your physical form can melt into the light and you will become invisible to those around you.

■ **The KEY of Hollow Earth is to tune into the blueprint of the planet.**

■ **The SOUND for this Golden Cosmic Key is the cosmic orchestra of all the sounds.**

■ **The COLOUR is azure blue.**

The Cosmic Era of Atlantis

Each out-breath of God lasts 26,000 years. This is a time of creation when things are being developed and expanded on Earth. Towards the end of the out-breath anything outstanding is brought to a conclusion, karma is balanced, the outmoded starts to collapse and this is what our planet and universe is currently experiencing. Then the in-breath commences and all is called back to the Godhead. During this period the old is dissolved or transmuted.

2012 marks the end of a cycle of ten out-breaths. This is known as a cosmic era, which lasts 260,000 years.

The last Golden Age on this planet occurred during Atlantis. An entire continent was set aside for the Atlantean experiment, which lasted for 260,000 years (10,000 years to set up plus 240,000 years in operation and 10,000 years to debrief and learn the lessons.) The cosmic era of Atlantis ends in 2012.

At the end of each out-breath there is an in-breath. At the conclusion of this entire cosmic era in 2012 the in-breath will last for eleven years until 2023. There is a nine-year pause, then the next out-breath begins and a time of creation commences again.

After 2032 there will be a fresh blueprint for Earth, for humanity and for the Universe, so that another Golden Age can start at a higher frequency than the previous one. We offer you the Keys to the Universe so that you can help to bring this about.

~ The blueprint of Golden Atlantis ~

The golden time of Atlantis, the 1,500-year period when the frequency on the planet was the highest it has ever been, was the last time that the light truly shone on Earth and the planet was bright. It was called a Golden Age because the light that radiated from everyone and the Earth itself was golden. The blueprint of Golden Atlantis was of a completely relaxed existence where everyone understood the animals, nature and the Earth. Everyone held a fifth-dimensional frequency, so that they co-operated for the highest good and lived in total harmony. They shared according to need, helped and respected each other and honoured the land.

The blueprint of that time is held in Hollow Earth, and the animals and birds are emerging now, imparting it to us. The songbirds, for example, are singing to us about the amazing possibilities we hold. The animals that have a fifth-dimensional frequency are coming up and living in a fifth-dimensional way, demonstrating this higher way to us.

~ 12 spiritual chakras and 12 strands of DNA ~

At the time of Golden Atlantis the twelve spiritual chakras of all people were open, awake and radiating. This meant that their twelve strands of DNA were fully active, so that they had spiritual and psychic gifts beyond our comprehension. Not only was everyone clairvoyant, telepathic and clairaudient, most people could levitate, heal, tune into the information in crystals and talk to the angels and unicorns. The Magi could fly, the High Priests and Priestesses travelled intergalactically to other star systems. They developed and used awesome spiritual technology, which was attuned to the highest good of the planet.

~ The angels of Atlantis ~

Angel dolphins and the angels of Atlantis who hold the wisdom of that era, are amongst us again and are transferring the knowledge to us through telepathy and other means. More people are beginning to remember their gifts and talents. Old natural, drug-free, healing methods are returning. Crystal wisdom and power is once more being harnessed.

~ The Great Crystal ~

Within the Temple of Poseidon in the centre of Atlantis was the Great Crystal containing the knowledge and wisdom of Atlantis. It also served as a portal. The Great Crystal now lies within the centre of the Bermuda Triangle and is one of the portals to Hollow Earth, see Key 29.

■ **The KEY of Atlantis is to relax deeply and honour the animals and the Earth.**

■ **The SOUND is the clarion call inviting everyone to live in the fifth dimension.**

■ **The COLOUR is gold.**

EXERCISE: *Visualization to honour the animals and the Earth*

1. Find a place where you can be quiet and undisturbed.
2. Light a candle to raise the vibration if possible.
3. Close your eyes and relax.
4. Ground yourself by imagining roots going from the soles of your feet deep into the earth.
5. Place Archangel Michael's blue cloak of protection around yourself.
6. Visualize yourself walking in a beautiful place in nature.
7. Picture the wonder of the soil, the rocks, the insects, the leaves, the roots and everything else.
8. Imagine what is happening with the rocks and crystals at a deeper level.
9. Let animals from all over the world come to you in your visualization and see the wonder of them.
10. Know that the more you honour, respect and admire the animals and the Earth the more you access this Key to the Universe.
11. After a while return to the place where you started your walk, bring your awareness back into the present moment and open your eyes.

EXERCISE: *Awareness walk*

- Go out into your garden, a park, the countryside or to the sea.
- Look at the wonder of every natural thing that you see whether it is a tree, a flower, a shell, a rock or the water. If possible touch them.
- Mentally acknowledge and thank every one of them for doing their part.

Lemuria

L emuria was the civilization before Atlantis. Beings arrived from all the universes to take part in the Lemurian experience and they all held the deepest love for the Earth. They were harmonious, fifth-dimensional and complete in themselves. They were androgynous, without sexuality and also had a great desire to heal the planet and the right energy to do this. However, the Lemurians were etheric, not fully in a body and did not physically step onto the land. In that sense they were like angels but vibrating at a fifth-dimensional frequency.

From our earthly projection we see the Lemurians as people on Earth, tall, with blond hair and blue eyes. But they were one huge energy, which wafted into different areas of the universe, affecting and healing the places they touched. They were a vast light force from all over the universes that worked in different places in various ways to heal.

They were all linked to the four ascension planets, stars and constellations, Neptune, Orion, Sirius and the Pleiades. The Lemurians also drew down the light and love of God through the cosmic heart into the Earth.

The Lemurians gathered the divine qualities from the energy fields of Earth and the auras of many planes of existence, stars, planets and constellations and added this to pure Source energy. When they focused this awesome light onto the planet it solidified and created the Lemurian crystals. They placed the crystals into the Earth and the light from them poured into the ley lines, so that the Earth was lit up from inside. The land was unconditional love.

In the film *Avatar*, when the Na'vi step onto their land in Pandora, their footsteps light up with love from their planet. However, it did not light up when Earthlings who were not in tune with their world walked on it.

The Lemurians touched Earth but also many other stars, planets and constellations, setting their healing crystals of incredibly pure energy in many places.

The crystals contain energies that bring forward and unlock what is needed to help the stellar world or the whole of creation at any given time. For example, if you are ready to work with the dragons to help the planet they would open the door to the dragon kingdom. If you are aligned to Petranium they would attune you so that you can access the energy you seek. You may need to use Lemurian crystals to draw forth a quality in someone. This quality may then be used to touch a project until there is a vast ripple effect, which is limitless and expansive. The Lemurian crystals must be used wisely because their effect continues to spread, touching many in its wake.

The Lemurians connected to Earth with the specific purpose of forming healing crystals for us. These crystals were specially formulated to help us through the transition to the New Golden Age. We can use their properties for many things including the healing of the planet itself. These crystals were the only evidence the Lemurians left of their presence, it was their intentional legacy for us.

Mother Mary was one of the cosmic beings who oversaw the Lemurian influence on Earth.

~ Grounding the energy of Lemuria ~

There was a period at the end of the Lemurian era, when the early Atlanteans had already arrived, before the Lemurians finally withdrew, and both civilizations co-existed. These first Atlanteans, who stepped physically onto the land were etheric and loving enough not to cause a frisson.

Eventually the Aborigines arrived on this planet to ground the energy of Lemuria. They were in a physical body, but their energy fields did not contain the unconditional love that Earth was familiar with and so at first they caused an imbalance. Much later in the time of Golden Atlantis however, the Aborigines were influenced by the Atlantean experiment – even though they were not part of it – and they learned to love the Earth unconditionally.

The cosmic portal in Hawaii, which is activating the great crystal of Lemuria and returning the wisdom it holds, is already opening.

■ **THE KEY of Lemuria is to connect to Source and bring your energy into balance with the true unconditional love of the Earth.**

■ The SOUND is a low hum connecting the four ascension planets.

■ The COLOUR is white-gold.

~ Lemurian self-healing with crystals ~

Self-healing is needed more and more now as our lower energies are surfacing because our frequency is rising. Make sure that you have no personal expectations for the outcome of the healing.

1. Use only pure ethically sourced Lemurian quartz crystals, which you can buy from a good crystal shop. They do not need to be cleansed for they are self-cleansing.
2. This is something that you need to do with other people, so that you can receive their feedback. When they hold the Lemurian crystals they bring them to life.
3. You look into your crystal as if it is a mirror – but remember we do not always see the truth about ourselves.
4. The others look into their crystals for you and they see, sense or feel what needs to be healed for you. When they have done so they lovingly tell you.
5. Ask the crystals to clear what needs to be cleansed or healed.
6. Visualize yourself connecting with the beating heart of the cosmos. This helps you accept whatever is cleansed or healed.

~ Lemurian crystal healing ~

Using a Lemurian crystal comes with a huge responsibility. Giving Lemurian crystals to someone without full explanation is like giving youngsters a motorbike and showing them how to ride it without impressing on them the correct way to use it. Lemurian healing energy has ten times the power of Reiki and spirit will not let us learn about healing with the crystals unless we are totally ready to use them with integrity.

Lemurian healing came from the deepest love and was always about the planet though it can be sent to individuals too. The energy is never sent by a single person. Where two fifth-dimensional people get together, they can focus the energy of the crystals into the Earth.

EXERCISE: *Visualization to connect with Lemurian energy*

1. Find a place where you can be quiet and undisturbed.
2. Light a candle to raise the vibration if possible.
3. Close your eyes and relax.
4. Ground yourself by imagining roots going from your feet deep into the earth.
5. Place Archangel Michael's blue cloak of protection around you.
6. Ask Mother Mary to come to you and picture her placing you in a ball of soft pink light.
7. Imagine you are part of the wondrous Lemurian energy.
8. You are holding a huge Lemurian crystal wand and you enter the Earth.
9. With your wand you are lighting up all the Lemurian crystals within the Earth until you can see our planet glowing and shimmering from within.
10. Take your wand and travel the cosmos lighting up the Lemurian crystals on other planets.
11. Stand back and see the entire universe glowing and shining with healing light.
12. Separate yourself from the Lemurian energy.
13. Then bring your awareness back into the room and open your eyes.

EXERCISE: *Lemurian walk*

The energy of Lemuria is white-gold. The Lemurians loved the Earth and all of nature and this walk will help you attune to that.

1. Find somewhere outside, in your garden, a park, the hills, the woods or by the sea.
2. For a while focus on breathing in love from the cosmic heart.
3. Then reach further into God and bring white-gold light down through you.
4. Sense you are leaving white-golden footsteps on the Earth. Then visualize them being lit up by the love of the Earth, so you are leaving a trail of love and light.

Mu

Many people talk of Mu as Lemuria and think the name is an abbreviation. However, Mu was an older civilization before Lemuria, which was also centered in the Pacific Ocean.

The people of Mu were of the fourth to fifth-dimensional consciousness and were not as evolved as the Lemurians. They had not taken on any physical form, and there are no remains.

The people of Mu tended the trees and plants and also worked with crystals but much less so than the civilization that followed. They were happy to be here and experience Earth, to connect with the animals and touch on the physicality of this plane, but they had no burning desire to heal the Earth like the Lemurians.

Although the people of Mu did not have the same depth of passion for nature and healing as the Lemurians, they had nevertheless huge love for the Earth and the four ascension planets, stars and constellations, Neptune, Orion, Sirius and the Pleiades.

~ *Sound mountains* ~

Those who love mountains recognize that they are alive and that they are entities in their own right. Like every living thing they emit a sound and that of the mountains is the high, clear note of angels singing. The person who coined the expression, "the hills are alive with the sound of music" was certainly attuned to this. The people of Mu were particularly attuned to the mountains.

The third Key is the sound held within the mountains of the world. Certain mountains or mountain ranges, like the Alps, send out exceptionally pure tunes, which affect everyone in the region. Mountains like those in Afghanistan contain lapis lazuli, emeralds and other gemstones, which emit their own notes and expand the range of the music of the mountains in this area. Where the energy of the earth is heavy, the notes are flat and discordant and need to be brought into harmony with the music of higher possibilities.

In Hollow Earth, within a blue aquamarine flame of Mother Mary and Archangel Michael's merged energy, the beings of Mu are holding the love of the five planets, stars and constellations, Earth, Neptune, Orion, Sirius and the Pleiades equally in wonderful healing light.

It is also the task of the beings from Mu to hold the Metatron Cube within Hollow Earth. This is where the love energy, the heart of the Metatron Cube is found. The divine blueprint of every star, planet and constellation is held within its hollow centre. Mu connects Hollow Sirius, Hollow Pleiades, Hollow Orion, Hollow Neptune and Hollow Earth. Within Mu in Hollow Earth is held the wisdom of the other four stellar connections, as well as Earth. It is all encapsulated in an etheric Metatron cube.

■ **The KEY of Mu is bringing together the wisdom of all the planets.**

■ **The SOUND is that of wind singing through the trees and music in the hills.**

■ **The COLOUR is pale yellow.**

EXERCISE: *Visualization to connect to the wisdom of the planets*

1. Find a space where you can be quiet and still, without being disturbed.
2. Light a candle if possible and dedicate it to connecting the Hollow centres of Neptune, Orion, the Pleiades, Sirius and Earth.
3. Close your eyes and breathe deeply. Let go of the outside world and relax.
4. Ground yourself by imagining roots growing from your feet deep down into the earth.
5. Place Archangel Michael's blue cloak around you, to protect yourself.
6. Imagine you are in the centre of Hollow Earth, in a beautiful natural paradise.
7. Invoke the beings of Mu and feel them around you.
8. You can see a huge blue aquamarine light in front of you.

Within it you can sense Mother Mary and Archangel Michael radiating healing and love.

9. Imagine you are travelling in the blue light to the centre of Hollow Sirius and hold the animals in the light. Breathe in the love.
10. Then move to Hollow Orion in the blue light and experience their paradise. Breathe in the love.
11. Then to Hollow Pleiades. Breathe in the love.
12. Then to Hollow Neptune. Breathe in the love.
13. Bring all the love and healing energy back to Hollow Earth and fill the heart of the Metatron Cube with it.
14. Thank the beings of Mu for helping you and exchange light with them.
15. Then bring yourself back into waking reality.

EXERCISE: *To listen to the song of the hills*

1. Dedicate this exercise to connecting with the energy of Mu.
2. If possible go to a hilltop and sit quietly. If not find a picture of a mountain and look at it.
3. Listen to the song of the hill or mountain and hum or sing it. If you find this impossible act as if you can hear it; then sing whatever comes to you.
4. Thank the mountain and receive its blessings.

Petranium –
The Origins of Africa

Petranium was the ancient civilization, pre Lemuria and Mu that seeded Africa and the African races. The great Ascended Master, Afra, a seventh-dimensional being who has energy similar to that of an Archangel, oversees Africa. While in a physical body he was male, but now he is androgynous. This is what Afra said to Kathy,

> 'I am of the planet. I walk by the people in Africa. I try to help them sense and feel that which is beautiful and pure and bring back the light of the Golden Age. Equally my energy is part of the Earth. It is in the crystals and soil and rocks, in Hollow Earth and the stars. However, my energy is not of Earth. It energizes the Earth. It enhances its qualities and brings out the properties that are necessary for animals and plants to survive. I am a light from afar which spreads through the pores of the planet to help in every way necessary. My force is like a finger of light from my home planet to Earth and stays with Earth.'

Afra works with Serapis Bey who helped setting up the pyramids after the fall of Atlantis. They both continue to oversee this continent.

Originally, the beings in Africa who formed the civilization of Petranium came from all over the universes, bringing knowledge from their planets in order to light up Earth. When Africa was first set up, there were already some beings on the other side of the globe in Asia who arrived in advance of those who came to Petranium. They responded to the same clarion call to come to Earth and they are still connected with our planet though they have never become physical.

The vast, varied landmass of Africa has always been here. In early times it was well covered with moist, green and vibrant vegetation. Every single plant was healthy. The land was magical. It was alive. This was the Golden Age of Petranium.

Originally, groups of people settled in various parts of the continent, for every area had different energy and purpose. The beings that first came here understood how to work with the planet, its earth, air and water. They even intuited how to embrace fire when it occurred.

Some of the first settlers knew how to work with the light and the crystals of Earth, especially how to help the crystals shine this light far and wide as a signal to other stars, planets and galaxies in this Universe for it showed them how Gaia was feeling.

Others worked with the water and understood how to bring its qualities to everyone. In those times water did not lie randomly. Nor did it fall because of the cycles of the planet. It was held.

Those who came to the continent worked very closely with cosmic beings and together they were able to direct clouds so that the water fell when and where it was needed.

In those times they knew how to feel the Earth; today we no longer have any concept of how to do this as they did. We have forgotten how wonderful, fragile and nourishing this soft layer on the surface of the Earth is for every one of us. They understood it.

The people did not mine the elements and minerals in the soil as we do now. They enhanced them by merging their own energy with that of the soil. In this way, by working with the water, they were able to share the elements and minerals far and wide.

Africa could still return to this wonderful state if those living there could reconnect with their innate knowing and reignite it. Then they could once again merge their energies with those cosmic beings who support this continent.

In the ancient times they understood how the stars, planets and moon drive the cycle of life. By asking and learning how, the life-giving properties of water could be used better once again.

The early inhabitants of Africa were small. They did not need a tall stature to achieve what they did for their auras were so vibrant and bright that height was of no significance. At first they were more energy than flesh.

There was no competition between the different areas. They all worked together to share their knowledge and experience for the greater good.

Golden Africa held a light that was alive and strong. Now the memories and the wisdom are held deep within the core of the land, yet they can be released and recaptured. Kumeka, my guide, tells us that we will not find the answers by trying to rationalize and understand the information. It has to be lived and the beings of the angelic realms are prepared to support us with this. Lemurian healing will help people to do this and this will assist in bringing new balance and awareness. The first step is to tame your mind. Then allow that knowing within your mind and brain to fill your aura. The Cosmic Masters now want us to expand.

The beings of Petranium were not contained within a body until they touched our Earth. Their energies were as small or as large as they needed to be. The life force on our planet is strong and heavy. Currently, as our frequency rises, we feel more tired and our bodies ache more. That is why we unconsciously limit our energy so that we feel lighter in our physical body. The cosmic beings tell us that it is time now for all on Earth to return to the high level of energy that we sustained for such a long time during the African and other Golden Eras. If we work with them they will help our bodies to accept the energy easily. They know it is a challenge but they are all here to help us.

When they worked as one with the cosmic ones, the crystals, the top layer of the earth, the water and the air, the light was incredibly bright. All life was in vibrant harmony but gradually, over many millions of years, this changed. The original ones found it more difficult to sustain the connection to their home stars and became separate from their influence. As they became denser, they took on the form of human beings. Their skin became darker because of the food they ate and the then temperate conditions where they lived. Their feelings and emotions became stronger until they became sexual and reproduced.

When beings first connected with the Earth in Africa they were more spiritual than physical. They were etheric like the Lemurians. However, unlike the Lemurians they eventually became physical beings. When they were etheric they were connected with their home stars, planets and universes. It was possible for them to live for thousands of years.

During the transition period as they were becoming more physical, the people lost the ability to keep Earth nourished. At that time their life spans varied, for many were able to return to their etheric bodies, dipping in and out of human bodies. Others could not and they had longer periods in a physical body so they did not live as long as those who returned to the etheric pool. When they finally lost all connection to their home planets, their frequency was still of the seventh-dimension, so they remain amongst us, invisible to those who are currently incarnate.

There are still thousands of the original seventh-dimensional ones in Africa. They are everywhere and go where they are most needed. If we were to open up we would sense their presence but as we hold our energies close and tight, we block ourselves and prevent this from happening.

The seventh-dimensional ones are helping the citizens of Africa reconnect with the land. They try very hard to help them feel their expanded selves, for the knowledge is still there waiting to be used. It will take a while to nourish the soil again but it is possible.

In more recent times people have felt the Original Ones but they cannot understand properly what it is that they can sense. They are scared of them, though they do not know what they are afraid of any more. They really have nothing to fear. They think the seventh-dimensional beings are gods but they are, in fact, their ancestors.

Some of the recent Africans have been trying to bring harmony back to the soil by encouraging people to follow the natural ways. They have done so by frightening people with threats from the 'gods' and must now seek inspirational ways to achieve their purpose. When the people link with and co-operate with the cosmic beings who fully understand how to work with elements and elemental beings, the ancient wisdom will return.

In addition the seventh-dimensional beings are all assisting the portals to wake up.

~ Africa after Atlantis –
The Dogons ~

The Dogons originated from Lakumay, an ascended planet of Sirius. At the fall of Atlantis, the High Priest Ra led his tribe to Egypt and part of it moved further south to Mali, where they became the Dogons.

The Dogons listen well. They are very wise beings who keep their connection back through time very well. They understand about the existence of the original seventh-dimensional beings who hold the light of Africa and they embrace their wisdom. They enable the wisdom from Lakumay to be anchored on Earth.

However, they are limited by their physicality and emotions, which often prevent them from sharing their knowledge. Because third-dimensional people surround them, it is hard for them to spread their wisdom and trust that others will receive the knowledge wisely. If people, wherever they are, would listen to them, not just hear them but truly listen they would learn a great deal.

~ White lions ~

White lions incarnate at special times in Africa and they are doing so now. They hold the ultimate level of trust. They are happy to shine brightly, stand out from the crowd, state very strongly what they stand for and not be scared of the consequence. They carry that light which shines across the whole of the universes, the light that is the energy of everything and everyone, the Christ light. They are bringing it to our world for the New Golden Age.

I was awed to meet white lions and feel their extraordinary energy, when I did research for one of my earlier books, The Web of Light, *the third title in a trilogy of spiritual novels.*

~ South Africa – the Solar Plexus of the planet ~

South Africa is the spiritual solar plexus chakra of the planet. In individuals and the planet the solar plexus draws in fear and transmutes it. When the chakra becomes fifth-dimensional it glows pure gold and radiates wisdom.

The Earth's solar plexus chakra, South Africa, is already fifth-dimensional but it is processing negative energy from the whole world. That energy is not held there. It is transmuted and given back as positive light but the chakra fills up again so quickly that it cannot glow. However, this will change after 2032.

When I was in Thailand I took a photograph of a magnificent Orb of Archangel Uriel who is in charge of the development of the solar plexus of the planet. The Orb was golden and several of its chambers were open, with pure Source light radiating through them. We were told that it had just transmuted all the negativity it had picked up and was pristine. Since then I have seen many Orbs of Archangel Uriel that are brown. These had taken in negativity, which had not yet been cleansed. That is currently the permanent state of the world's solar plexus chakra in Africa. As we approach 2032, there will be less fear for it to hold.

~ *The goal of Africa* ~

Ultimately the goal of Africa, like that of all countries, is to light up the planet. It holds within its physical make-up a connection to Hollow Earth, as well as crystals and memories, which will bring tremendous wisdom to us all. When Africa connects with its divine potential, it will enable reconnection to the cosmic beings and this will, in time, allow a symbiotic relationship with elements of fire, earth, air and water once more.

There is much cleansing of the human ego to be done before this can occur. It is only when we become fifth-dimensional that we can understand the natural essence of our planet and use the immense power wisely for the highest good.

~ *Abundance for Africa* ~

Abundance will flourish in Africa when the Africans embrace the truth. The portal of Table Mountain holds an understanding of abundance consciousness. When the people of Africa trust their wisdom, their energy and who they truly are, the country will flourish. The portal of Table Mountain is radiating trust as an energy that all can absorb. As they accept it they will start to increase their self-worth and this will ultimately bring prosperity. It is possible that by 2032 everyone will be fed.

Cosmic beings are all the beings and people who are fifth-dimensional and above. They include the angels and spiritual masters from other planets. They hold the summation of the knowledge of the universe that we need to call on. If we were working with the seventh-dimensional ancient ones and their energies we could reverse global warming, heal the ozone layer and return the planet to its healthy state.

■ **The KEY of Petranium is to reconnect with the ancient knowledge, wisdom and light held within the core of Africa – and to fuse with the energy of the Elemental Masters. People will then be able to work with the elementals to direct the water of the planet, so that they can alter the weather for the greater good of nature and life.**

■ **THE SOUND of ancient Africa is drumming as if it was the heartbeat of the planet.**

■ **The COLOUR is purple green.**

EXERCISE: *Visualization to connect with Golden Africa*

1. Find a space where you can be quiet and still.
2. Light a candle if possible and dedicate it to Golden Africa.
3. Close your eyes and breathe deeply. Let go of the outside world and relax.
4. Ground yourself by imagining roots going from your feet deep into the earth.
5. Place Archangel Michael's blue protective cloak around you.
6. Imagine yourself moving into the time of Golden Africa.
7. Stand with your feet in the rich fertile earth, surrounded by the green beauty of the land.
8. Connect with the vibrant harmony of the continent.
9. Then be aware of the presence of one of the Original Ones, a mighty seventh-dimensional being, holding all the wisdom and knowing of Africa.
10. Merge your energy in that of the Original Ones and feel the wonder of being in the seventh dimension.
11. See yourself walking through modern Africa and touching the people with wisdom.
12. Know that you have made a difference and experience the good feeling this engenders.
13. Thank the Original Ones.
14. Bring your awareness back to the room and open your eyes.

EXERCISE: *To connect to the white lions*

1. Take yourself out into nature, the sea, the countryside, the forest or even a park.
2. Call upon a white lion to walk with you as your protector and friend.
3. Be aware of the high frequency of this magnificent white creature, who carries the Christ light of unconditional love.
4. As you attune to the white lion's energy you may find higher thoughts coming into your mind.
5. Ask questions and let responses from the white lion come to you.

Angala

This refers to the time aeons ago when Earth was first being formed. It was the period during which God was gathering the energy to create our planet.

In the divine mind there was the thought of Earth and the protection of the angels to hold it safe. That was Angala.

At first it was a naked planet full of love, just like a newborn baby – a precious, fragile creation. It received the full love and attention of Mother/Father God and the angels. Later, trees were seeded from the mind of Source. They did not come from another universe. Trees are ancient wise sentient beings holding the knowledge of their local areas.

The original thought in the mind of God had a seventh-dimensional blueprint but the wondrous and unique concept that was added was free will. Every creature that evolved here or arrived from another plane of existence could shape its own destiny.

Because time is not linear but all things are happening now, Angala is an instant of limitless potential. It is an eternal birthing time when anything and everything is possible.

When you comprehend this concept you can bring forward a new idea, tune into the energy of Angala, the first moment of Earth and the entire universe will support and enfold your project. There are no limits.

- The KEY of Angala is a complete trust in Source that you can create something unique and wonderful.

- The SOUND that attunes you to this energy is the sound of birth, the heartbeat.

- The COLOUR is pure white.

EXERCISE: *Visualization to connect with the energy of Angala*

1. Find a space where you can be quiet and undisturbed.
2. Light a candle if possible and dedicate it to Earth.
3. Close your eyes and breathe deeply. Let go of the outside world and relax.
4. Ground yourself by imagining long roots growing down from you deep into the earth.
5. Place Archangel Michael's blue cloak of protection around you.
6. Visualize the Earth as it was when it was being birthed, precious, delicate and vulnerable.
7. See it develop as grass, plants, trees and animals appear.
8. All is in perfect harmony. All is working in co-operation and peace.
9. Feel the glory of the divine intention.
10. After a while, bring your awareness slowly back into the present and open your eyes.

EXERCISE: *To manifest a vision*

1. Decide on a vision you wish to bring into your life.
2. Draw a circle to represent Earth.
3. Round it draw angels, which do not have to be perfect! Just know that they represent the highest, purest light and are holding your vision safe and protected.
4. Within the circle draw a picture or symbol of something you wish to birth.
5. Birth and energize your vision with humming, chanting, prayer or action.

The Aborigines

Most of the ancient cultures arose from Atlantis but the Aborigines arrived during the time of Lemuria. The original Aborigines came from another planet in this universe, stepping down their energy through Sirius. They incarnated, grounding the energy of the Lemurians.

The Aborigines held a deep love for the Earth and understood it intimately. They knew how to tread lightly on it without hurting its ecosystem. The trees of Australia, which were created from the mind of God, were seeded as the first Aborigines incarnated. At the same time the animals unique to this continent, including snakes and reptiles arrived from other planets and universes for this particular experience. At that time all animals were totally harmless for every being lived in harmony and co-operation.

The portal of Uluru offers access to Hollow Earth. The Aborigines are the link connecting Hollow Earth to the Sun.

They are predominantly right-brained and carry the divine feminine on Earth. The women embrace the highest feminine qualities of wisdom, creativity, empathy, intuition, togetherness, sharing, co-operation, nurturing, compassion and receptivity to spirit. The practice of the oral tradition enables the essence of messages to be passed on in stories, encouraging continuity. Because sharing is promoted the Aborigines take collective responsibility for the land and this too enables the continuation of their culture.

The divine feminine is balanced by the divine masculine which is enhanced by their special connection to the Sun and enables the higher characteristics, like strength, courage, power to protect, order and structure, to be maintained.

In effect, the Aborigines bring in the divine masculine of the Sun to the divine feminine of Mother Earth. When the right and left-brain are totally in balance and harmony we find a sense of peace and safety and are one with the universe. This is what the Aborigines are teaching us.

> *For my sixtieth birthday I travelled round Australia for six months. I held the vision of meeting and talking to Aborigine elders. Within three weeks I had been given a contact to some elders who lived in Cooktown, the northeast tip of the continent, which at that time was way beyond the road system. It took me two months to make my way up there and on the way I was invited to visit an Aborigine school where no white people were allowed. That was fascinating and it felt like an honour. When I reached Cooktown and talked to the elders I was deeply impressed by their humility, compassion, forgiveness and wisdom. I write about them in **The Codes of Power**, my second spiritual novel.*

■ **The KEY of the Aborigines is to listen to the sound of the didgeridoo while feeling your feet in the Earth and love in your heart.**

■ **The SOUND is that of the didgeridoo balancing the masculine and the feminine.**

■ **The COLOUR is green.**

EXERCISE: *Visualization to learn from the wise Aborigine elders*

1. Find a space where you can be quiet and still.
2. Light a candle if possible to raise the vibration.
3. Close your eyes and breathe deeply. Let go of the outside world and relax.
4. Ground yourself by imagining roots reaching down from your feet deep into the earth.
5. Place Archangel Michael's blue cloak around you for protection.
6. Picture yourself treading lightly on the red earth of Australia in perfect harmony with the trees.
7. Take time to connect with the native animals, koalas, emus, kangaroos, crocodiles and snakes. What do they have to teach you?
8. Ask a wise Aborigine elder to come to you and tell you what you need to know.

9. Thank them for sharing their wisdom with you.
10. Then bring your awareness back to your present surroundings and open your eyes.

EXERCISE: *To balance your masculine and feminine energies*

1. On a sunny day go outside and bathe in the light.
2. If possible walk with bare feet but in shoes if this suits you better. Feel the earth under you.
3. Contemplate the way in which you use your masculine energies: strength, courage, decisiveness, power to protect others, order, structure, linear thinking and strategic outcomes.
4. Contemplate the way in which you use your feminine energies: wisdom, creativity, empathy, intuition, togetherness, sharing, co-operation, nurturing, compassion and receptivity to spirit.
5. Mentally ask the sun and the earth to bring your yin and yang into perfect balance.

Alternatively you can do this exercise sitting or lying down while listening to the didgeridoo.

The Incas

One of the twelve tribes descending from Atlantis that each hold Keys to the Universe was the Incas. They were on Earth but not of Earth.

At the fall of Atlantis, the great High Priest, Thoth, led his tribe to the North West of South America, where they became the Incas. These first Incans originated from Venus and for a long time they kept their original skills and understandings. They all practised telepathy, levitation, energy healing and oneness.

They poured love and wisdom into the creative gold work they crafted so that each piece held knowledge as well as healing power. They worked with copper and, like the Aztecs, they also used Orichalcum, a pink gold metal, the frequency of which vibrates with the Sun and carries its qualities. Copper resonates with their planet of origin, Venus.

Thoth taught that there is a correspondence between every single thing in the universe and when each is in harmony the universe is in harmony.

Because nature is built according to sacred geometry, each medicinal plant contains a specific geometric structure, as does every part of the human body. When the mental, emotional or physical body is in perfect synch with its divine blueprint, radiant health will result. All the High Priests and Priestesses of the Golden Era of Atlantis understood which herb had the same geometric structure as, and vibrated perfectly with, each part of the body. If eaten, that herb would seek out the blueprint of the damaged organ within the body and align, heal and regenerate it.

Every cell emits a sound and when all the cells of the body are in perfect health and attunement with the divine plan, your personal song is glorious. Due to past or current life traumas you may have suppressed certain notes that will be missing from your repertoire. By listening to and sounding those specific notes you can re-tune yourself to the total wellbeing of your original blueprint.

The Incans used energy to heal by bringing the chakras into alignment. They understood the powers of visualization and could create total health by visualizing it. These and other forms of energy healing will be the basis of maintaining longevity, health and happiness in the future, in the New Golden Age.

■ **The KEY of the Incas is understanding the use of energy to bring everything into harmony, alignment and wholeness.**

■ **The SOUND is a whoop of joy from the heart and humming from the heart.**

■ **The COLOUR of the Incas is gold.**

EXERCISE: *Visualization to become whole, healthy and perfect*

1. Find a place where you can be quiet and relaxed.
2. If possible light a candle or place some flowers nearby to raise the vibration.
3. Close your eyes and ask the mighty High Priest Thoth to over-light your visualization to connect with your true divine blueprint. You may sense his presence as you slip into a reverie.
4. Picture yourself as vital, slender and relaxed.
5. You may like to see yourself walking or running freely and easily. Are you on a beach, in the countryside or up a mountain?
6. Notice that your hair is shining, bouncy and alive. Your skin is clear and your eyes radiant. Feel your life force.
7. Be aware that your heart is strong and pouring out love. You are also receiving love from nature, the elementals and the angels.
8. See every part of your body working easily and effortlessly.
9. The cells are lighting up as you attune to your divine perfect blueprint and you may feel laughter bubbling up inside you.
10. What do you need to eat, drink, think, say and do to maintain this wonderful state of vitality, health and happiness? Take time to decide.
11. Spend a few minutes being aware of the whole, healthy and happy, perfect you.

12. Then open your eyes, return to the present and enjoy the feeling of your divine blueprint.

EXERCISE: *Visualization to bring yourself and the entire universe into harmony*

1. Find a place where you can be quiet and relaxed.
2. If possible light a candle or place some flowers nearby.
3. Close your eyes and thank the High Priest Thoth for bringing you into harmony with the entire universe. In his presence you feel totally safe.
4. Breathe light into every part of your body.
5. Imagine you are standing on a hill on a clear moonlit night.
6. Be aware that all your chakras have opened wide and light from Source is pouring into your crown, through your whole body and into the ground below you. Feel the peace and the harmony this brings.
7. Sense a golden thread connecting you to the moon and the stars.
8. The golden thread is connecting you to the trees, to the people, the animals.
9. Little golden threads are connecting you to the elementals.
10. The threads are linking you to the rocks, the mountains, the oceans and rivers.
11. You are in the centre of millions and millions of connections. Send peace and harmony out along them.
12. Experience the oneness of a harmonious universe and take this feeling back with you when you open your eyes to your current reality again.

EXERCISE: *To be at peace*

1. Find somewhere out in nature and if possible touch a rock, a tree or some water.
2. Breathe in the peace and love of nature until you feel really comfortable.
3. Look at the sky and breathe that peace and love to the sun or the moon.
4. Imagine the stars that are there waiting to come out and breathe peace and love to them.
5. Breathe peace and love to the mountains, rocks, oceans and rivers.

6. Breathe peace and love to the trees and flowers, people, animals and elementals.
7. Relax and open yourself to receiving peace and love in return. Breathe it in.
8. Notice how you feel now that you have exchanged peace and love with all these parts of the universe.

The Aztecs

The Aztecs were another of the twelve tribes with the energy of Atlantis, holding a Key to the universe. At the fall of that ancient civilization, the great High Priestess Isis led her tribe to South America, where they became the Aztecs. Like the Incas, these first Aztecs originated from Venus and brought with them love and wisdom.

They had a very strong understanding of and connection with the stars, especially Venus and this enabled them to create their Aztec calendar that starts with the birth of Venus and ends in 2012. The pyramids they built contained advanced knowledge and information about Venus and the stars in our universe and how their energies link and balance each other in cosmic harmony.

The walls of the Temple of Poseidon in Atlantis were covered in orichalcum, a pink gold copper, which was found in the Atlantean mountains. The Aztecs and the Incas both worked with this pink gold metal. Orichalcum vibrates with the sun, which adds to its power and brightness. Copper resonates with Venus and holds love.

The Aztecs radiated qualities of love, joy and delight in life and they passed this energy into their crafts and their daily life. They were able to connect their hearts to the hearts of animals, trees, rocks and the whole of nature and this enabled them to understand their symbiotic relationship. While the Incas were physical healers, the Aztecs understood soul healing. They each knew the right path for their soul and followed it. They intuited the right foods to clarify the soul and kept themselves in balance and in constant alignment with their divine blueprint.

It is very interesting that at school certain topics grab your interest much more than others and these I now know resonate with our soul's purpose. Kathy was particularly interested in the Aztecs, yet at the time she had no concept of her pathway, which she now knows has to do with helping people connect to their soul so they can walk in their truth for the greatest good.

■ **The KEY of the Aztecs is understanding and loving who you truly are so that you are in tune with your divine blueprint and the planet.**

■ **The SOUND is silence followed by a gentle ting on cymbals.**

■ **The COLOUR is pink gold.**

EXERCISE: *Visualization to feel accepted and loved exactly as you are*

1. Find a place where you can relax and be undisturbed.
2. Remind yourself that you deserve this time for your spiritual growth and connection.
3. Light a candle or place flowers by you, if possible, to raise your energy.
4. Close your eyes and let your lids feel heavy and comfortable.
5. Breathe away any tension in your body.
6. See yourself out in the universe, alone, peaceful and at one with yourself.
7. Then the golden light of Source appears and enfolds you totally, so that you feel accepted and loved exactly as you are. You know you are totally protected.
8. Relax for as long as you need to experience this and for the energy to saturate the cells of your being.
9. When you feel accepted and loved just as you are, open your eyes and smile at the wonder of the universe.

EXERCISE: *To clear your soul pathway*

1. Find a piece of paper and some crayons.
2. Think about the Aztecs as you do the following drawing.
3. A pyramid, coloured gold and pink in the centre.
4. Above it the sun.
5. Draw a tree, a flower, an animal and a rock. Then link them with lines to each other, the sun and the pyramid.
6. As you do this let a thought come to you about the right diet, exercise, activity to clear your soul pathway.

The Babylonians

Another of the twelve tribes of Atlantis, that hold Keys to the Universe, was the Babylonians. At the end of Atlantis, the great High Priest Horus led his tribe to Babylon. They carried with them a vast knowledge of the seasons, the power of the sun and the properties of water.

When they arrived in their new location the land was green and beautiful and the Babylonians tried to maintain this as it was. In order to do so they worked with the elementals. They had an honouring, loving and symbiotic relationship with them, so that the humans and elementals tended the land and the plants together.

In addition, they truly respected the water. They blessed it and kept it pure, honouring it with ceremony. El Morya was a master living in this place at the time. He recognized the cosmic properties of water, fully understood its hidden esoteric qualities and power and taught this information to the people. They were thus able to use water to cleanse, purify and heal.

The former Atlanteans helped the locals to learn about irrigation. Through their knowledge and close co-operation with the elementals the tribe developed the Hanging Gardens of Babylon, which became one of the Seven Wonders of the World.

They brought with them great skills and trained people to design creative buildings and fashion beautiful crafts.

The Babylon citizens were merchants and tradesmen and Horus and his tribe from Atlantis taught them to trade with honour and integrity in accordance with the Spiritual Laws.

~ The Spiritual Laws ~

There are 33 spiritual laws and three transcendent laws: see Key 47 for further illumination. I also describe these laws in a simple and easily understandable way in *A Little Light on the Spiritual Laws.*

■ **The KEY of the Babylonians is to work with what nature provides for the greater good and to understand and apply the spiritual laws.**

■ **The SOUND is that of running water.**

■ **The COLOUR is crystal with green aquamarine.**

EXERCISE: *Visualization to connect with the wisdom of Horus*

1. Find a place where you can be quiet and relaxed.
2. Light a candle if you can.
3. Close your eyes and let yourself relax.
4. Invite the High Priest Horus to connect with you and breathe in the pure crystal-clear light with green aquamarine as he protects you.
5. Relax deeper as Horus reminds you of the true wonders of water and the exact power of the spiritual laws.
6. Visualize a desert and imagine an aqueduct being built there. See water criss-crossing the desert, bringing it to life.
7. Watch the greenery spreading, trees springing from the Earth, flowers cascading over hills.
8. Know that you have the power to generate life.
9. When you have integrated this knowledge, return your awareness to the room and open your eyes.

EXERCISE: *To bless and honour the water*

– Bless, love and thank the water you drink today.
– When you bath, shower or use water be consciously aware of its cosmic properties and thank it for cleansing and healing you.
– Hold your hands out to the rain, or over puddles, lakes or rivers you see and bless the water with love.

The Egyptians

The great High Priest Ra was head of one of the twelve Atlantis tribes, which held the Keys to the Universe, and at the fall he led his people to Egypt. The subsequent High Priests became the Pharaohs and they held the knowledge from Atlantis to build the Great Pyramid. The Master Serapis Bey and Universal Angel Metatron supervised this from the spirit world and added the cosmic information, which is stored within the Pyramid at a fifth-dimensional level. They were helped by the Universal Angel Butyalil who is in charge of the cosmic currents.

~ The Great Pyramid and the Sphinx ~

The Great Pyramid is linked with Sirius and Orion and brings in wisdom from those stars and constellations, then passes it through to Hollow Earth. Originally, the top of the Great Pyramid was crowned with a huge rotating crystal, held in place by energy that poured up from Hollow Earth and down from Sirius and Orion. These energies created an equal and opposite force that enabled the crystal to maintain its balance.

It was a seventh-dimensional cosmic portal, which was a safe meeting place for beings from Hollow Earth and seventh-dimensional beings from the universe.

By the time the pyramids were constructed, the energy on the planet was mostly third dimensional and higher beings needed a safe haven where the lower energies could not impact on them. The purity of the light within the portal helped them feel oneness.

The Sphinx is the other part of the entry portal to Hollow Earth. The statue has always contained the energy of Source and still does. God force is infused in the stone and radiates from here to the whole world. You just have to think about it to receive an extra boost of divine energy. Within the Sphinx are held the Akashic Records for our universe, maintained within a fifth-dimensional energy.

~ Healing ~

The Egyptians brought with them from Atlantis medical knowledge and information about all natural therapies. They understood the divine healing properties of medicinal plants when used correctly, as well as the power of the mind or crystals when correctly applied.

When enough people reach the fifth dimension and can tune into the Great Pyramid again, new forms of healing using the special properties of plants, crystals, water, colour, massage and many other therapies, will spread from here.

~ The six-pointed star ~

This is one of the most powerful and beneficial of the ancient Atlantean spiritual symbols, which was utilized by the Egyptians. It is composed of an upward triangle taking Earth to Heaven and a downward triangle, bringing Heaven to Earth. In addition, if you visualize it filled with the gold, silver and violet flame of transmutation and mercy, then invoke the Gold Ray of Christ to pour over it, it is a very powerful way to transmute the old and raise the energy of a place, person or chakra.

*I was asked by my guide Kumeka and the Universal Angel
Metatron to place the six-pointed star filled with the gold
and silver violet flame and surrounded by the golden Christ
Light in some woods where the energy was very dark. It used
to make me shiver when I walked along that particular path.
The symbol transformed the cold, dark feeling in that place in
a magical way.*

*I also visualize it over my twelve chakras sometimes and
again I can really feel the difference. This is something I often
do when walking quietly in nature.*

■ **The KEY of the Egyptians is to connect to the six-pointed star,
bringing Earth to Heaven and Heaven to Earth.**

■ **The SOUND is a high-frequency, high-pitched sound that con-**

nects the pyramids to the stars. It is like a grasshopper and the gentle whoosh of angel wings.

■ The COLOUR is royal blue, which is a rich blue with some red. This is a regal, majestic colour, in which red adds energy and life force to the noble blue.

EXERCISE: *Visualization to heal with the six-pointed star*

1. Find a place where you can be relaxed and undisturbed.
2. Light a candle, if possible, to raise the vibration.
3. Close your eyes and relax deeply.
4. Place a violet six-pointed star in the Gold Ray of Christ over each of your chakras, breathing in the energy as you do so. Alternatively you can place a huge one over your entire body.
5. Visualize the six-pointed star over the Great Pyramid to energize the symbol.
6. Then place the energized six-pointed star wherever you want, over places or people to transform and heal the energy.
7. When you have finished, open your eyes knowing you have performed a worthwhile act of service.

EXERCISE: *To draw the six-pointed star*

1. Draw a six-pointed star.
2. Either colour it in violet or outline it in that colour, while you think of the violet flame.
3. Place rays of yellow gold around it and contemplate the Gold Ray of Christ, of unconditional love.
4. You can make your star as large or small as you wish to.
5. You can leave it in a room to clear the old and raise the light or you can place the star on a map, on a photograph of a person, on a picture of your home or write a location or person's name on the star. This is a very powerful way of helping to clear a blockage in the ley lines. Your intention will direct the energy where you want it to go.

EXERCISE: *To walk the six-pointed star*

1. Outline the six-pointed star in chalk, with string or stones.
2. Walk the outline, while invoking the gold silver and violet flame and the Gold Ray of Christ.
3. Imagine the energy searing deep into the Earth, helping to clear and awaken it.

The Innuit

At the fall of Atlantis the great High Priest Sett took his tribe to Alaska with one of the Atlantean Keys to the Universe. They were shamans, able to go through the veils to retrieve information. They also had a complete comprehension of the working of the stars and planets. They could, for example, read them to discover the optimum time to travel. They understood their effect on the weather.

Like the Babylonians they had a particular connection with the element of water and had an intimate understanding of its life-giving properties and how important it was for fish, seals and polar bears.

They had a symbiotic relationship with animals and communicated with them on a telepathic level. Like the Native Americans they connected with the higher selves of animals before they took one to eat. The soul of the animal agreed to surrender its life to maintain theirs and in offering this sacrifice received sacred blessings. Whether fish or warm-blooded animal, they blessed it before they ate it and gave thanks for its life.

The Innuit keep the ancient stories of Atlantis and they still tell, dance and sing them, so that the essence of the messages are passed on in perpetuity.

Because they live in the purity of the ice and snow the Innuit maintain their original connection to the divine and are attuned to their true guidance.

■ **The KEY of the Innuit is to remain pure and connected to your guidance.**

■ **The SOUND is that of water dripping from an icicle.**

■ **The COLOUR is the blue-white of pure ice.**

EXERCISE: *Visualization to connect to guidance*

1. Find a place where you can be quiet and undisturbed.
2. Close your eyes and imagine a pure blue white light enclosing and
    purifying you.
3. Ask the High Priest Sett to come to you. Sense his presence and
    know that he is helping you.
4. Call an animal to you and visualize or sense it in front of you.
5. Thank it for coming. Then empathize with that animal. Listen to
    what it has to tell you.
6. Respond telepathically if that is required.
7. When the communication is over, bless it and visualize it happy,
    honoured and respected in its natural habitat.
8. Thank Sett for helping you.
9. Bring your awareness back to the present and open your eyes.

EXERCISE: *To honour the gifts of the Earth*

–   Whatever you eat today, whether it is plant or flesh, think of its
    life, the nutrients it holds, the way it has developed in the sun
    and rain and the qualities it is offering you. Bless it before you eat
    it and spend a few moments thanking it for its service to you.

The Native Americans

At the fall of Atlantis, the great High Priest Imhotep led his tribe to what is now the United States to form the Native American culture. They hold one of the Keys to the Universe.

Originally it was the Cherokees who carried the secrets of Atlantis. Gradually they spread their influence across the land mass and other groups were formed all of whom carried part of the sacred wisdom.

They practised shamanism and had the ability to move beyond the veils. This enabled them to use their understanding of dream catchers and how to work with them. One of their gifts was that of soul retrieval and part of their healing practice was to ensure that missing or lost aspects of a person were returned to their rightful place, so that the individual could participate fully and comfortably in this experience on Earth.

The Native Americans are keepers of the ancient wisdom of the Earth. They have always known and taught that Earth does not belong to us but we are entrusted to be its custodians. They honour the land and all things living on it and in it, and have always had a special relationship with animals, respecting them and treating them as brothers. They also understood that humans, animals, sun, moon, stars and everything are One.

■ **The KEY of the Native Americans is to honour the land and all things living on and in it.**

■ **The SOUND is the fast drum of the heartbeat of the land.**

■ **The COLOUR is red and brown.**

EXERCISE: *Visualization to connect with Imhotep and the Native American culture*

1. Find a place where you can be quiet and undisturbed.
2. If possible light a candle.
3. Close your eyes and breathe into your limbs imagining them becoming heavier and very comfortable.
4. Ask the High Priest Imhotep to come to you and sense him wearing his huge feather headdress.
5. He is placing a feather headdress on your crown. Notice if it feels familiar.
6. You are wearing moccasins and are walking very lightly on the earth as you follow him.
7. He leads you to a horse and invites you to connect telepathically with it. Feel the bond between you. Send it love.
8. The horse is returning your love and you spring onto its bare back, knowing you are safe.
9. As the horse moves beneath you, you can feel the wind in your face, the sun on your back. The sky is vast and blue. The trees and plants are sending energy to you.
10. Take time to feel that you are one with all of nature. You all depend on each other and love each other.
11. Feel the oneness.
12. When you are ready, thank Imhotep, then return to the space you started from and open your eyes.

EXERCISE: *Walk to honour the land*

- Give yourself time and space so that your full attention is on the land and nature.
- Touch a tree and honour the spirit of that tree. Offer it thanks and a blessing.
- Feel the grass, sand or earth under your bare feet. Bless it for supporting you and notice how it feels. Thank it for serving you.
- Sense the energy of the plants and flowers. Is it winter? If so how do they feel when their energy is withdrawn. Is it spring? How do they feel to be bursting into life? Thank them and enjoy them.
- Listen to the birds and watch them fly. Connect your heart to their hearts.
- If possible stroke an animal with reverence and respect. Telepathically

let it know that you are aware it is a wonderful soul on it own path of ascension.

- Move your fingers through the water of a pond, river, lake, sea or even a puddle. Be aware this is a special element with cosmic properties that connect all things. Thank it.
- Each time you do this exercise it will be different.

The Kahunas of Hawaii

At the fall of Atlantis, the great High Priest Hermes, who was later known as a God in the Greek culture, ruled a tribe that he took to Hawaii. This tribe became the Kahunas and they hold a Key to the universe.

Hermes is the guide to the underworld, which in this case is Hollow Earth. He is very linked to the Earth Star and offers you access from there to Hollow Earth. If you connect with him and the Universal Angel Sandalphon in your Earth Star Chakra, he will help you go deeper into Hollow Earth. In meditation you can ask him to take you round all the different areas. You can also ask him to conduct your spirit on a tour while you are asleep.

The Kahunas brought with them a powerful link with the dolphins. Hermes helps you to meet the dolphins on the inner planes to connect to their joy and knowledge – and also the angel dolphins to bring back the wisdom of Atlantis. He assists those who are ready to travel inter-galactically with the dolphin light. This is a fifth- to seventh-dimensional energy, depending on your needs at that time. You call in silver dolphin energy to surround you, then invite Hermes in and ask to travel with him. The dolphin energy will protect you. He takes you to places where you ask to go and assigns one of his angels to wait for you, while you do your work.

Hermes was an Olympian God and he encourages the pursuit of excellence and the fine-tuning of the body through sport. The ultimate aim of this is to bring everyone together for worldwide peace and harmony.

Hermes is known as the Patron of Boundaries and he looks after travelers who cross them. In this he works with Archangel Raphael, who is the Angel of healing and abundance as well as travelers. Together they enable people to journey easily on Earth in their physical bodies.

They help those explorers who have the right mindset, for they humbly wish to discover the wonders of God's creation.

~ Huna Prayer ~

Hermes is a messenger god and he co-operates with the Universal Angel Sandalphon to take the messages in our prayers up to God. The Kahunas are remembered for their Huna prayers, which are one of the most powerful forms of supplication. It was Hermes who set out the rules for them. The Huna prayers use spiritual law to outline an effective form of asking. The Spiritual Realms say that it is now time for everyone to access this wisdom and understand how to make a Huna prayer.

The Law of Prayer reminds us of the importance of faith, trust and belief. It says that, if you ask Source for something and you totally trust that it will be granted, your faith triggers a response from the heart of God and the angels are already bringing your request to you.

However, many people outwardly trust but inwardly doubt, because the subconscious mind often contains beliefs, memories or feelings that block us from receiving our good. The subconscious, conscious and the superconscious minds all need to be aligned for a prayer to be fulfilled. The Huna Prayers use the might of all three aspects of the mind to create a powerful form of supplication.

Hermes discovered that our conscious mind must raise enough energy to push the prayer through the subconscious to our Higher Self or soul. The Kahunas love to dance, chant and clap and this increases the life force or energy to affect this.

He knew that once God has received the prayer, your soul can then connect with the angels and masters who help to activate it.

The Kahunas remind us to say the prayer three times daily for thirty days. The repetition impresses our subconscious mind like an affirmation and helps to open up the route to success.

■ **The KEY of the Kahunas is to attune to the wisdom of the dolphins and explore Earth and the far reaches of the universe.**

■ **The SOUND is that of the conch shell.**

■ **The COLOUR is silver blue.**

EXERCISE: *Visualization to travel with Hermes and the dolphins into Hollow Earth and the universe*

1. Find a place where you can be quiet and undisturbed.
2. Light a candle if possible.
3. Close your eyes and relax.
4. Call in the dolphin energy and feel the silver blue light surround you. Breathe it in and relax deeper into it.
5. Imagine roots going down into your Earth Star chakra and take your consciousness down into this beautiful space below your feet.
6. Here you meet and greet the tall Universal Archangel Sandalphon.
7. Now the High Priest Hermes appears and you greet him too.
8. Ask them to take you down into Hollow Earth and show you what you need to see. Take time to explore this wondrous space.
9. When you have seen all you need to experience here and wish to travel inter-galactically, ask Hermes to take you to a planet where you can serve or experience.
10. Be aware of the dolphins' silver blue light even more strongly now.
11. Follow Hermes out into the universe and visit a star or planet where you can be of assistance. Do what you need to do.
12. When you have finished, one of Hermes' angels will conduct you back to the place where you started.
13. Relax for a while to integrate your experiences.
14. Thank Hermes, Sandalphon and the dolphin energy.
15. Then open your eyes and ground yourself back in waking reality.

EXERCISE: *To work with the Huna Prayer*

1. Purify yourself to clear the path to your Higher Self. Do your purification exercise each day before you say your Huna Prayer.

    Here are examples of ways to purify yourself:
    a. Physically shower while calling on the cosmic properties of the water to cleanse you.
    b. Ask the unicorns to pour their light over you.
    c. Invoke the gold and silver violet flame to transmute anything that needs to be dissolved.
    d. Ask Archangel Gabriel to clear and purify your energy fields.

2. Address your prayer to the Beings you wish to work with. You can ask one angel or master – or several. It is usual to address them as Beloved. You might like to start your prayer with: 'Beloved Jesus, Allah, Mary, El Morya, Archangel Michael.' You may prefer to address your prayer, 'Beloved God,' or 'Beloved Buddha.' It is up to you.

3. Write down clearly what you wish to manifest for the highest good. Make sure there are only positive words in your prayer. Start with 'I ask and pray with all my heart and soul' to add even more force to it.

4. Raise your energy with a dance, visualization, clapping, singing or in any other way.

5. Say your prayer aloud three times. End with, 'So be it. It is done,' in a firm, clear voice.

6. Tell your subconscious mind to take the prayer to your Higher Self with all the energy it needs. Picture it shooting up and out of your crown.

7. Relax for half a minute or so after this. You might like to say OM quietly.

8. Sit with your palms up and open. The Kahunas use the words, 'Lord, let the rain of blessings fall.'

9. In the next few days or weeks listen for a response. If you intuitively feel you need to take action, do so. If you want to make more than one request in your prayer you can do this as long as it is simple. Include in your prayer something for which you are grateful. If you materially change your prayer, start again with the thirty-day process.

The Tibetans

At the fall of Atlantis, the great High Priest Zeus, who was later known as a God in the Greek culture, ruled an Atlantean tribe, which he took to Tibet with one of the Keys to the Universe.

Zeus brought with him the qualities of stillness, peace and harmlessness to all creatures. Gradually the Tibetans developed them into the Buddhist religion. They were aware that when you radiate harmlessness, every creature around you feels totally safe and nothing will hurt you.

Zeus directly influences the whole of the modern Middle East and when the cosmic portal in Mesopotamia opens he will be working with it to help spread stillness, peace and harmlessness in the area. The Tibetans will spread their light to bring the people of the Middle East into spirituality.

Zeus was the King of the gods and the god of sky and thunder. He has a vast understanding of the elements that create the weather. He worked with the original beings who came to Africa during the time of Petranium to help control the climate.

He is working with the Australians and beings from other planets so that when the portal of Uluru opens he will be able to assist them to understand the rain and other elements and direct them to make more of their continent fertile and abundant.

He is co-operating with Poseidon to oversee the worldwide cleansing of the planet, utilizing the elements of air, water, fire and earth to influence weather conditions.

As I am writing this in the UK I should be in Dublin but my flight was cancelled because of the eruption of a volcano in Iceland, which was releasing ancient karma from the land with fire and air. It grounded all the aircraft in Europe as a wake-up call to show us how vulnerable we are.

We are not masters of the air and must tune into and respect the elements.

In addition this tribe is working with the Universal Angel Fhelyai, angel of animals, to open the hearts of people to enable them to understand animals. It is time that humanity knows that animals are all on their own individual soul journey to ascension just as we are. Many of them are highly evolved. Some incarnate to learn as humans do. Others are here to teach.

Zeus collaborates with Quan Yin on the beauty of creativity that expresses spirituality in mosques, temples, churches and all places of worship in the whole world. In addition he uses his power to protect people and groups, especially those who are standing out and doing spiritual work.

The energy of Zeus and his tribe is particularly strong in the mountains of Tibet where they work with Archangel Gabriel to spread purity, clarity and joy.

■ **The KEY of the Tibetans is to live in compassion, harmlessness and peace and enter the Silence.**

■ **The SOUND is that of chanting.**

■ **The COLOUR is white.**

EXERCISE: *Visualization to spread peace and harmlessness*

1. Find a place where you can be quiet and undisturbed.
2. Play gentle rhythmic music if possible.
3. Relax and close your eyes.
4. Ground yourself by imagining roots growing from your feet deep into the earth.
5. Place Archangel Michael's blue cloak of protection around you.
6. Focus on your heart. Breathe in pure white peace and breathe out harmlessness.
7. Feel yourself become still and silent.
8. Visualize yourself in the pure mountains of Tibet and breathe in the silence.
9. Ask the High Priest Zeus to come to you. Sense his energy.

10. Go with him to the Middle East and radiate peace and harmlessness everywhere.
11. Travel with him to other countries and touch the hearts of people, telepathically reminding them to honour and respect animals for they have souls and feelings.
12. Thank Zeus for letting you serve with him.
13. Return to the place where you started and open your eyes.

EXERCISE: *Walk to spread harmlessness*

1. Walk in nature where it is quiet and if possible silent.
2. Breathe in the peace of nature.
3. Radiate harmlessness to all the animals and birds.
4. Next time you meet people silently radiate harmlessness to them.
5. Notice how your heart feels when you do this.

The Mayans

A t the fall of Atlantis, the great High Priestess Aphrodite led her tribe to South America, where they became the Mayans. Like the Incas and Aztecs the first Mayans originated from Venus and brought with them love and wisdom.

They are famed for their knowledge of astronomy and mathematics, which enabled them to calculate the Mayan calendar, covering the time span 3114BC to 2012AD. Their wisdom was programmed into their cosmic pyramids, which they built, accurately aligned to the stars and galaxies. They were calibrated to connect with Venus and Andromeda on 21st December 2012 to release the incredible information about Atlantis as well as stellar knowledge programmed within. The Mayans call this cosmic moment, forecast for 2012, 'Creation Day'. The prophecy says that the force touching the pyramids on that day will result in a rebirth of the solar consciousness of humanity and will accelerate the ascension of individuals and the planet. Aphrodite and Thoth are working together to bring their ancient wisdom forward for the New Golden Age.

Aphrodite as High Priestess of the tribe that became the Mayans, fashioned with the power of her mind one of the twelve crystal skulls of Atlantis. She created the skull that contained all the love, incredible cosmic wisdom and practical higher knowledge of the Mayans.

Aphrodite works with Lady Venus from the planet Venus to enable pure love to flow from there to the hearts of people throughout the world. She tries to bring peace where it is needed and she co-operated with the Intergalactic Council to release the Mayan skull in 1927 in an endeavour to maintain peace in Europe.

As a being of love she also focuses abundance on the Earth. The Mayans had vast and advanced knowledge of nature, farming and the healthy growth of trees, crops and plants of all kinds. She helps to cross-pollinate species of plants to keep their strength and it is her task to keep the world blossoming and blooming. She continuously reports to Source about the needs of plants, trees, animals and people on our planet.

Aphrodite and the Mayans help to transform emotional love into pure love. All that she does for plants she does for humans. She helps couples see the best in each other so that their relationships flower.

■ **The KEY of the Mayans is to hold love in your heart and breathe it out to nature, so that the world continues to grow and blossom.**

■ **The SOUND is that of tinkling laughter and tinkling bells and the flute.**

■ **The COLOUR is pink.**

EXERCISE: *Visualization to blossom with love*

1. Find a place where you can relax quietly.
2. Light a candle, if possible, or place some flowers to raise the vibration.
3. Close your eyes and relax.
4. Imagine a beautiful pink light flowing from Venus into your heart, until your heart is so big that pink love surrounds you.
5. Visualize a bare cherry tree and watch the pink blossom bursting out all over it.
6. Send that pink to friends and family and visualize the love blossoming.
7. Send it now to acquaintances and strangers and sense love blossoming for them.
8. Send it to your garden or park or the countryside and picture it alive with flowers and the trees flourishing.
9. Picture all the stars, people, animals, trees and beings of nature connected with pulsating vibrant pink love.
10. See that network of love integrating into your heart and your essence.
11. When you feel nourished and radiating, bring your awareness back into the room and open your eyes.

EXERCISE: *To energize the love of Venus*

1. Go outside on a clear night and look at Venus in the sky.
2. Breathe in the energy and imagine your heart growing bright pink as love blossoms within it.
3. Then breathe out that love to all the stars in the sky.
4. Now breathe love to the people everywhere, picturing their hearts opening.
5. Then breathe love to the animals, trees, plants and the whole of nature. See everything open up and blossoming.
6. Thank Venus and the Mayans for holding the energy of love on Earth.

The Mesopotamians

At the fall of Atlantis, the great High Priest Apollo, who was later known as a God in the Greek culture, ruled a tribe, which he took to Mesopotamia. This tribe also holds a Key to the Universe.

Apollo is connected to the sun and has a radiant, golden, masculine energy that affects all those who tune into him. A gentle understanding softens his power, force and might so all that he does is balanced. Therefore he demonstrates the masculine ideal. He is sometimes called The Archer because his masculine energy enables him to focus his thoughts powerfully in order to manifest for the highest good. He is a god of light and truth, bringing the good, wise and excellent into the world for us.

He is often shown with a lyre and indeed he plays music with the angels over humanity to bring about peace. This music affects people at a cellular level and creates a masculine feminine balance within them. When these two aspects are balanced in every cell the whole body comes into harmony. He works with Fekorm, the Universal Master of Music and also with Thoth to help the cells of all living things to sing in tune.

Apollo directed the building of the great cosmic pyramid in Mesopotamia, which has been destroyed and is no longer visible. However, it is still there energetically, connected to the stars and ready to wake up in 2012. Apollo encoded within it information about Atlantis and also knowledge about the stars that form the basis of Western Astrology.

The tribe's understanding about the movement of the stars was the foundation for their understanding about irrigation. As a result they used water not just as liquid but recognized the cosmic properties to nurture the plants. They are bringing this knowledge forward after 2012 to help us. It is time for us to return deserts to verdant and abundant areas.

There are three feminine energies that are helping Apollo to bring the waters of the planet into harmony and balance.

These are:
- Artemis who is associated with the moon.
- Isis who was overlit by the Universal Angel Mary in many life-times. She was Ma-ra in Lemuria and set up the Mystery Schools; a High Priestess of Golden Atlantis giving virgin birth to Horus; and Mary, who gave birth to Jesus.
- Heda who comes from another universe and is the twin flame of Fekorm, Universal Master of Music. Heda and Fekorm tend to work together.

Apollo is associated with poetry because he works with the resonance, harmony and rhythm of the cosmos.

This tribe brought from Atlantis vast amounts of knowledge about the medicinal plants. Apollo works with them, directing people to use the right herbs to bring the organs of the body into balance. The resonance of the herbs brings the diseased part of the body into perfect ease and harmony.

■ **The KEY of the Mesopotamians is to bring everything in the cosmos into resonance and harmony.**

■ **The SOUND is the sound of the stars singing and the plants growing.**

■ **The COLOUR is green gold.**

EXERCISE: *Visualization to bring all into rhythm and harmony*

1. Find a place where you can be quiet and undisturbed.
2. Play gentle rhythmic music if possible.
3. Relax and close your eyes.
4. Ground yourself by imagining roots leading from your feet deep into the earth.
5. Place Archangel Michael's blue cloak of protection around you.
6. Invoke Apollo to come to you and feel his radiant gold light surround you.
7. Ask him to take you out into the cosmos to feel the harmony, rhythm and resonance of the entire cosmos.
8. Visualize yourself with Apollo out amongst the stars.

9. Be aware of the connection of the stars to each other and the music between them.
10. Notice how all the planets are sending love to each other.
11. Feel the entire universe singing and resonating in harmony.
12. When you have taken this experience in, let Apollo bring you back to your body.
13. Let this harmony flow and move in every cell of your body.
14. Then thank Apollo, return your awareness to the room and open your eyes.

EXERCISE: *To bring a plant or tree into divine harmony*

1. Play beautiful rhythmic music to a plant or tree.
2. Tune into Apollo and bless some water with cosmic joy. Then water your plant or tree.
3. Thank the entire cosmos for helping this plant or tree.

The Greek Culture

The great Atlantean High Priest Poseidon, who was later known as a God in the Greek culture, ruled a tribe, which he took to Greece at the fall of Atlantis. They also hold a Key to the universe.

Poseidon brought with him from Atlantis the wisdom and knowledge to build one of the six great Cosmic Pyramids. He oversaw the building of the one in Athens, which is under the Parthenon. In it is encoded information about Atlantis and the influence of the stars on the tides and winds. This tribe understood the cosmic knowledge and knew how to navigate the planet by using them. They also charted the oceans.

After 2012 when the kundalini of the planet rises and triggers the stellar connections to the Great Pyramids, this information will come forward and enable us to move more easily with the flow. We will learn to travel in divine timing under optimum influences.

The people of Poseidon's tribe were great scholars: Within the great Cosmic Pyramid in Greece there is an etheric fifth-dimensional library. After 2012 fifth-dimensional people will be able to tune into it and draw out ancient knowledge by using yellow light from their minds. It will help them to accept the information into their right brain and then transfer it into their left-brain for processing.

Much of the special information the Greeks brought from Atlantis is about natural medicine and healing. They understood the exact note of every organ and what influenced it to stay in perfect harmony. This could be attained for example by attunement to a particular star, flower or tree. Eating a specific herb or special food might be the secret. Or it may be that the colour or sound that resonated with that part or pressure on a particular place could enable the body to achieve true alignment.

They developed and worked with advanced forms of healing the mind so that it influenced the physical.

They had in-depth knowledge of crystals and even in Atlantis worked with Lemurian healing wands as well as the qualities of all other crystals. For example, it was Poseidon who worked with Archangel Raphael to focus his ray into the mountains of Afghanistan in order to form high-frequency emeralds to cure people. He chose this particular location because it is connected to the healing constellation of Andromeda and the wisdom of Orion. In addition Afghanistan is the spiritual 'third eye' chakra of the planet and Archangel Raphael is in charge of the third eye chakras for the whole of humanity. When Afghanistan is ready in 2032, the third eye of the planet will radiate gloriously and enlighten the world. See the Orb of Archangels Raphael and Purlimiek below.

Poseidon works with Joules, the Universal Angel in charge of the Portal of the Bermuda Triangle where the Great Crystal of Atlantis lies. Together they watch over the tectonic plates.

- ■ **The KEY of the Greek culture is to develop the mind so that it can heal the body.**

- ■ **The SOUND is that of the harp connecting everything in the universe.**

- ■ **The COLOUR is mid-yellow.**

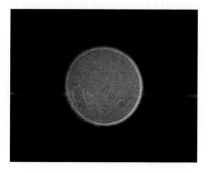

The Archangels Raphael and Purlimiek. This Orb helps you value the abundance that nature has to offer.

Photograph by Tracey Morais

EXERCISE: *Visualization to heal the third eye chakras of the people and the planet*

1. Find a place where you can be quiet and undisturbed.
2. Play gentle rhythmic music if possible.
3. Relax and close your eyes.
4. Ground yourself by imagining roots going from you deep into the earth.
5. Place Archangel Michael's blue cloak for protection around you.
6. Visualize yourself in the magnificent mountains of Afghanistan, the spiritual third eye chakra of the planet.
7. Call in Archangel Raphael to heal and bring abundance to Afghanistan.
8. Ask him to light up the emeralds in the mountains here.
9. Call in the unicorns and ask them to pour the pure light of enlightenment into this country.
10. See Afghanistan radiating light.
11. As it does so feel your own third eye light up.
12. Know that you have made a difference.
13. Return to the place from which you started, thank Archangel Raphael and the unicorns.
14. Then open your eyes.

EXERCISE: *To heal with sound and intention*

1. Find someone to do this exercise with and take it in turns.
2. Invoke Archangel Raphael and feel his bright emerald light enfold you.
3. Ask him to work through you and set the intention of healing your partner.
4. Place your hand on your partner, where they need healing or balancing.
5. Hum, chant or tone so that the sound vibration enters your partner's energy field.
6. Then change over.

The Maoris

The great High Priestess Hera, who was later known as a Goddess in the Greek culture, ruled another Atlantean tribe that, at the fall of Atlantis, she took to Fiji and then to New Zealand. They became the Maoris.

The Maoris were mystics and shamans, able to travel through the veils of illusion between the worlds. With her special wisdom Hera helps all who have shamanistic powers to travel into other planes of existence and bring back healing or lost parts of a soul. She works with the higher selves of power animals and enables them to connect with people they are attuned to.

Hera holds the Keys to the sacred secrets of the universe and unlocks the doors for people who are ready. She helps them to see into dimensions beyond this physical one, develop intuition and connect with the Powers of the universe, including angels.

Her sacred knowledge includes secrets of fertility and abundance and this will be particularly useful after 2012 for it will help with farming and enable us to feed people in a way that nurtures the Earth and honours animals.

There was a time in the Golden Era of Atlantis where people and animals served each other, while respecting their differences and honouring their uniqueness. She is helping to bring this back now.

She over-lights women, marriage and childbirth and she is assisting females to take their rightful place in society once more.

If a woman is apparently infertile and wants a child she assists them to prepare on every level, mental, physical, emotional and spiritual and then helps them to link to the right soul who is waiting to incarnate. There are those who long for a child but do not conceive and that is because their souls have decreed it is not to be their experience for this lifetime. She helps them to recognize and come to terms with this.

She works to expand the right brain of people, especially women, so that they can remember the stories, chants and songs, which contain the wisdom of the ancients. Recognizing the power of rhythm and sound, she places sacred spiritual energy within the chants so that the information and wisdom they contain is passed on through generations.

In this way she helps with the continuity of families and cultures.

■ **The KEY of the Maoris is to develop intuition and attune to the sacred mysteries of the universe.**

■ **The SOUND is that of clapping.**

■ **The COLOUR is mid-blue.**

EXERCISE: *Visualization to receive wisdom and healing*

1. Find a place where you can be quiet and undisturbed.
2. Light a candle if possible or play suitable music.
3. Relax and close your eyes.
4. Ground yourself by imagining roots going from you deep into the earth.
5. Place Archangel Michael's blue cloak around you for protection.
6. Ask the Goddess Hera to connect with you and you may sense or see her with you.
7. Ask her to take you out into the universe for wisdom, healing or to retrieve part of your soul.
8. Trust her to conduct you through the veil to the optimum place for your spiritual advancement.
9. Experience what you need and listen to Hera's guidance.
10. Thank her and let her bring you back to where you started.
11. Then bring your awareness back into the room, open your eyes and write down your experiences.

EXERCISE: *To explore your background*

– Explore the background of your family or culture and learn more about the history. If possible you can ask older relatives where your forebears lived and what their work or interests were. Perhaps you can discover the reason why the people of your culture undertake

certain practices or believe in particular things. For example, you may learn why they have their hair in a certain fashion or wear specific clothes, or the underlying meaning of their devotional songs.
- Understanding these aspects of your culture enables you to understand more about yourself and the ancient wisdom you embody.

The Portals

To reach the stars, the angelic realms and the seventh dimension you either go through your Stellar Gateway chakra into the cosmos – or you go through your Earth Star chakra into Hollow Earth. Preferably you are able to do both. The deeper you take your consciousness into Hollow Earth the higher you can expand into the stars.

There are twelve entry and exit portals between Hollow Earth and the surface of the planet, which lead into the cosmos. Each of these is a Key to the universe.

The Great Pyramid and Sphinx, Egypt

The Great Pyramid is one of the cosmic pyramids built at the fall of Atlantis. It connects to Sirius and Orion while the Sphinx is the entry to Hollow Earth. So the light from Hollow Earth travels up from the Great Pyramid to the stars and down from them through the Sphinx into Hollow Earth.

The Sphinx acts as a portal, accessing information from Sirius, Orion and various other stars and planets. A fifth-dimensional tunnel underneath the Sphinx leads to the Great Pyramid of Hollow Earth, and this is where the Akashic Records, the records for the entire universe, are stored.

The Key is the merging of the information from the stars encapsulated within a sacred geometrical cone as it comes into the Sphinx. From below the cone of information comes from Hollow Earth to the Sphinx and this forms a figure of eight or eternal loop of divine wisdom.

■ **The KEY of the Great Pyramid and the Sphinx is to connect to the figure of eight.**

■ **The SOUND is the humming of the pyramid connecting to the universe.**

■ **The COLOUR is crimson red.**

EXERCISE: *Visualization to access information from the Akashic Records*

1. Find a place where you can be quiet and undisturbed.
2. If possible, light a candle to bring higher vibrations in.
3. Relax and close your eyes.
4. Ground yourself by imagining roots going from your feet deep down into the earth.
5. Place Archangel Michael's blue cloak of protection around you.
6. Take your consciousness into the Great Pyramid and up to Sirius and Orion, then down through the Sphinx into Hollow Earth, then back again. Follow this figure of eight a few times.
7. Feel the God force within the Sphinx as you pass through it.
8. Visualize yourself going through the fifth-dimensional tunnel from the Sphinx to the Great Pyramid of Hollow Earth. Then enter the pyramid.
9. With awe and reverence enter the great library where the Akashic Records are stored.
10. A master approaches you. Ask if you may access information that will enable you to grow spiritually.
11. The master leads you to an area where he invites you to sit. He hands you a special quartz crystal.
12. As you relax and tune into the crystal you receive a download of information. This may come as pictures, thoughts or just a sensation.
13. When you have finished return the crystal to the master and thank him.
14. Then come back through the tunnel to the Sphinx and out to the place where you started and open your eyes
15. Over the next few hours or days you may be aware of cosmic or personal information that you did not know before.

EXERCISE: *To unlock ancient wisdom through the figure of eight*

–   Draw out a figure of eight on the ground and walk it with the intention of unlocking the wisdom of Sirius and Orion for the highest good.
–   If you cannot walk it, draw a figure of eight on a piece of paper and run your finger round it, holding the intention of unlocking ancient cosmic wisdom.

Mount Shasta, California

One of the factors allowing the high frequency of the Golden Era of Atlantis to be maintained was a dome of crystal pyramids placed over the land. This contained the experiment and beamed great light into it. After the fall of Atlantis most of the pyramids were returned to the inner planes but one was moved into the etheric over the sacred mountain of Mount Shasta. This keeps the energy here clear and pure.

The retreat of Archangel Gabriel is in the etheric above Mount Shasta and he too keeps the entire area filled with white light. He is holding purity, joy and spiritual awakening for this area and will continue to do so as the cosmic chakra here opens in 2012.

The portal at Mount Shasta leads directly down into the Lemurian energy of Hollow Earth and then links up to the Pleiades. Pleiadean healing is brought through Mount Shasta to the surface of Earth and to Hollow Earth.

In one direction this portal is used by souls who live on the Pleiades to come to Earth or Hollow Earth. Angels from the Pleiades who want to visit Earth or Hollow Earth use it too. While they can access Earth by themselves and do not need to come through a portal, they move through this particular one into Hollow Earth to spread their knowledge about healing.

We were puzzled when we were sent an amazing blue Orb of a diamond shape, quite different from other ones, and then we were told that it was a being from the Pleiades bringing healing to the land. They are currently preparing particular areas for ascension. See this Orb on the next page.

In the other direction, our angels take souls from Earth through the portal to the Pleiades in their sleep if they want to learn about the Pleiadean healing methods.

Beings from the Pleiades can also teleport or travel in other ways but they do not use spacecraft.

The spirits of animals from the Pleiades travel through Mount Shasta. In addition the souls of Pleiadean animals, who are about to incarnate on Earth, use the portal to visit us before they finally make the journey to experience life on our planet. We have seen many Orbs of angels bringing spirits to reconnoitre potential families, their possible future parents and grandparents, brothers, sisters, aunts and cousins, before they make the final decision to connect with a mother. Many of these waiting souls take the decision very carefully indeed.

Sheep come from the Pleiades to offer us wool, comfort and healing through goodwill. Bees, who originate from this constellation, had no stings when they first came to Earth for they did not need to defend themselves. Stings were developed as the frequency went down. They pollinate flowers, show us how to live in harmony in a very ordered way and build according to sacred geometry. They give us healing through comfort and by offering their sweet honey. Pigs are also from the Pleiades and balance the ecology by eating leftovers. They are loved and respected for their intelligence and wisdom. They too are healers by offering their friendship and healing the land. Our task is to offer them respect and shelter.

Pleiadean healing Orb. This Orb is a being from the Pleiades bringing healing to this place to prepare it for ascension. When you look at it the Orb will bring your energy into perfect balance.

Photograph by Biljana Markovic

~ About Pleiadean healing ~

All Pleiadean healing is heart-centred but, as you will see from the Orb of a Pleiadean healer visiting this planet, their energy is the blue of the throat chakra. This is because they are healing with truth.

When I first visited Mount Shasta several people told me that their grandparents used to talk of Lemurians they met while they were walking out on the mountains. It was said they entered their homes through a tunnel into the Earth.

■ **The KEY of Mount Shasta is healing from the heart by enfolding people in pure love.**

■ **The SOUND is that of angels singing.**

■ **The COLOUR is blue-white.**

EXERCISE: *Visualization to learn about healing through the wisdom of the Pleiades*

1. Find a place where you can be quiet and undisturbed.
2. Light a candle if possible.
3. Relax and close your eyes.
4. Ground yourself by imagining roots going from you deep into the earth.
5. Place Archangel Michael's blue cloak around you for protection.
6. Ask Archangel Gabriel to visit you. Sense his pure white light around you.
7. Within his energy visualize yourself visiting the portal of Mount Shasta in wonderful snow-covered mountains. Breathe in the energy.
8. Ask Archangel Gabriel to take you through the portal to the Pleiades to learn about and receive healing from the Pleiadean angels.
9. Feel your heart opening and your cells filling with high-frequency blue light. Take as long as you need to experience this.
10. Thank the Pleiadean angels.

11. Return with Archangel Gabriel through the portal of Mount Shasta into Hollow Earth.
12. Spread the beautiful blue heart-based, healing energy along the ley lines.
13. When you are ready return with Archangel Gabriel through the portal back to where you started.
14. Thank him and open your eyes.

EXERCISE: *To appreciate the animals*

1. If possible go outside into the country and find a bee, sheep or pig. If this is not possible, look at a picture of one, or imagine one in front of you.
2. Breathe love from your heart to them.
3. Then telepathically thank them for coming to Earth and for all the service they have offered us.
4. Take a little time to appreciate and value them.

The Mayan Cosmic Pyramid, Guatemala

The great nine-step Mayan Cosmic Pyramid, which was built after the fall of Atlantis, is a portal, which is linked to Venus and also to the cosmic heart.

This pyramid draws through it the love of the cosmic heart into Hollow Earth, where Lady Gaia sends it into the planet and the Universal Angel Gersisa then spreads it through the ley lines. On Earth, when the stream of love comes in, it draws the darkness to it to be dissolved and this is currently causing some turmoil here by churning up stuck energies. Only unconditional love goes into Hollow Earth.

As the planet rises in frequency, Guatemala and the whole of South America will blaze with light.

The Mayan Pyramid is also linked to Sirius. The kundalini of the planet moved to Guatemala in 2008, coming into the influence of the higher aspects of Sirius, Lakumay, which aims to focus sacred geometry, so taking the planet into higher dimensions. The wisdom of Sirius is held within the ninth-dimensional Gold Ray of Christ.

■ **The KEY of the Mayan Cosmic Pyramid is to spread and focus unconditional love.**

■ **The SOUND is the hum from the heart that connects the crystal skull, stars and sacred geometry.**

■ **The COLOUR is pale crystal pink.**

EXERCISE: *Visualization to bathe in cosmic love and Christ light*

1. Find a place where you can be quiet and undisturbed.
2. Light a candle if possible.
3. Relax and close your eyes.
4. Ground yourself by growing imaginary roots from your feet deep down into the earth.
5. Place Archangel Michael's blue protective cloak around you.
6. Visualize yourself entering the Cosmic Mayan Pyramid and sitting in its centre.
7. Open yourself up to the ray of pure pink light pouring in from the Cosmic Heart and let it bathe you in wondrous love.
8. Then open yourself up to the Gold Ray of Christ pouring in from higher Sirius.
9. Be aware of the sacred geometric symbols coming into you.
10. Allow the pink from Venus and the gold from Sirius to flow through you down into the centre of Hollow Earth.
11. See Lady Gaia and the Universal Angel Gersisa take it and send it through the ley lines.
12. Picture the entire planet pulsing with pink and gold love.
13. When you have finished return to the place where you started and sense your aura also pulsing with pink and gold love. Notice how this feels.
14. Open your eyes and smile.

This is an excellent visualization to do before you go to sleep, so that the pink and gold love flow through you during the night. Your Higher Self will ensure you only take in what you can cope with.

EXERCISE: *To spread unconditional love through sacred geometry*

1. Find an atlas of the world or a local map.
2. Focus on your heart.
3. Draw a six-pointed star and colour it pink.
4. Hum from your heart and send the sound to the six-pointed star.
5. When it is full of energy place it somewhere on your map.
6. You can do this as many times as you want!

Agata,
Northern Russia

One of the most important, powerful and influential cosmic portals is opening at Agata, Northern Russia around 2012. It links to the Pleiades.

Kundalini is the essential life force of a plant. It holds all the information and energy needed for its growth and when it is ignited the plant starts to shoot up. The conditions in which a flower is planted, soil, shelter, sun, rain and the tender care it receives clearly affect its vitality. It is exactly the same for a person. When the time and conditions are right, our kundalini rises and we start to wake up and expand spiritually. All stars and planets follow the same system and when the planetary kundalini of Earth is ignited in 2012 we will all see rapid spiritual growth.

At the fall of Atlantis the kundalini of the planet was masculine and was held in the Gobi Desert by Sanat Kumara. It contained the low frequency energy of later Atlantis and this needs healing so that the planet can rise to ascension from 2012 onwards.

In 2008, Mayan shamans moved the kundalini to Guatemala where it has become a feminine energy, bringing balance to the planetary life force. However, the Atlantean aspect of the kundalini still needs healing. In their efforts to do this the Pleiadeans access the Atlantean energy in Hollow Earth through the portal at Agata, Northern Russia.

Now that the kundalini has moved from masculine to feminine and been taken to Guatemala, the Earth Star Chakras of everyone on the planet are coming into balance. The masculine force of the planet is relaxing and is being bathed in peace and healing. It is now changing from that of the fighting warrior to that of the peaceful warrior who works for the highest good with wisdom, while shielding the weak, poor and vulnerable.

The masculine force is starting to help people on Earth to take the highest possible decisions and is bringing back the knowledge necessary for the planet to transform into harmonious co-existence with nature, animals and the whole of humanity. It is protective by being peaceful, strong, courageous and divinely guided.

■ **The KEY of Agata is to balance the masculine and feminine energy to bring about harmonious co-existence.**

■ **The SOUND is that of a low soft gong rippling out into silence.**

■ **The COLOUR is Pleiadean blue.**

EXERCISE: *Visualization to heal and balance your kundalini*

1. Find a place where you can be quiet and undisturbed.
2. Light a candle if possible.
3. Relax and close your eyes.
4. Ground yourself by imagining roots going from you deep into the earth.
5. Place Archangel Michael's blue protective cloak around you.
6. Visualize yourself as a plant and take your roots into the soil, into your Earth Star chakra. How tall are you? What are your leaves like?
7. Now you wish to grow taller, so your roots must go deeper. Take them deep, deep into Hollow Earth.
8. Feel the warm sun and refreshing rain on you and watch or sense yourself grow.
9. Your roots are now receiving all that they need. Sense yourself growing up to Source now. How does this feel?
10. Separate yourself from the plant but still feel your roots are deep in the earth and your head in the heavens.
11. Ask the Pleiadean healers to heal and balance your ancient karma. Trust that this is being done. Thank them when they have finished.
12. When you are ready open your eyes, knowing that you have balanced your kundalini and have helped the planet to balance its kundalini too.

EXERCISE: *To be a peaceful warrior*

- Whether you are a man or a woman practise being a peaceful
  warrior today and help everyone co-exist in harmony.
  Examples: If your children are quarrelling or you are with people
  who are arguing, instead of shouting, stay strong, centred and
  peaceful so that they feel your energy and calm down. If you are
  with those who are turbulent and anarchistic, calmly hold your
  vision of peace and a higher outcome, then see how this affects
  their mood.

The Cosmic Pyramid in Greece

A fter the fall of Atlantis a cosmic pyramid was built in Greece; this has since been obliterated by an earthquake. However, the energy is still active. Long after its destruction the Parthenon was constructed on its site and this forms the portal. The higher wisdom from Orion pours through here into Hollow Earth, into the library of Porthologos in the City of Catharia, which contains all the original wisdom of this ancient culture.

All the animals that incarnate on Earth from Orion – cats, goats, red squirrels and rabbits – carry part of that wisdom in their energy fields.

~ The Spiritual Laws ~

There are 33 spiritual laws and three transcendent laws. The Key is the wisdom of Orion, which is about the spiritual laws of the Universe. The spiritual laws are great immutable energies that enable everything to work in perfect divine order. They are held energetically within the Greek pyramid under the Parthenon. The 33 spiritual laws were laid down by the High Priest Thoth in Atlantis. They were also taught by Horus who led the Babylonians.

The three transcendent laws were decreed by Source for they hold divine qualities, which override all other energies in the divine scheme.

~ The Spiritual Law of Attraction ~

Some of the spiritual laws can be used in the third dimension but there is a karmic consequence. They only work energetically in alignment with your soul in the fifth dimension. One such is the Spiritual Law of Attraction, which is so much discussed in our time. This Spiritual Law states: when you focus on what you desire without doubt or deviation it must manifest.

In the fifth dimension you only ask for a wish if it is for the highest good. You are prepared to hand it over to the angels and let it go if it is not in accordance with divine will.

Then it comes to you in a perfect divine way without attracting any karma. The Atlanteans knew this and used the law appropriately.

~ The Transcendent Laws ~

There are three transcendent spiritual laws, laid down by God, which supersede all other laws. These are based on very high-frequency divine energies, which transmute and dissolve all that is not love and light.

~ The Law of Faith ~

If you trust God to such an extent that you have total faith in an outcome it must come about. Faith allows the impossible to become possible. It opens the way for miracles. Listen to your intuition and trust it. That is the foundation for faith.

~ The Law of Grace ~

Unconditional love, compassion, mercy, forgiveness, open-hearted generosity and empathy are divine qualities, which confer grace. When you offer these qualities to others, you receive grace from the divine.

~ The Law of One ~

Duality is a teaching tool to encourage us to reach for the light. In the fifth dimension and above we know we are all part of God yet we are all different. We accept and honour the divine in others and ourselves.

■ **The KEY of the Cosmic Pyramid in Greece is to understand and follow the spiritual laws.**

■ **The SOUND is that of a gong getting louder to tune into the spiritual laws.**

■ **The COLOUR is a shimmering pearl.**

EXERCISE: *Visualization to receive wisdom from Orion*

1. Find a place where you can be quiet and undisturbed.
2. Light a candle if possible.
3. Relax and close your eyes.
4. Ground yourself by imagining roots going from you deep into the earth.
5. Place Archangel Michael's blue cloak around you for protection.
6. Visualize yourself sitting out in a beautiful place in nature.
7. You are approached by a cat, a goat, a red squirrel and a rabbit.
8. Each has wisdom from Orion to impart to you, so listen to what they have to tell you.
9. Honour their light and thank them for coming.
10. Then bring your awareness back into your waking reality and open your eyes.

EXERCISE: *To practise the transcendent laws of the universe*

– Contemplate the three transcendent laws: How can you demonstrate faith in your life? Where can you offer grace today? Can you see the divine in others?

The Great Cosmic Pyramid in Tibet

After the fall of Atlantis one of six great cosmic pyramids was built in Tibet by Zeus, containing the wisdom of Atlantis. It is linked to the spiritual aspect of Sirius, Lakumay, and holds one of the Keys to the universe.

The pyramid has now been completely destroyed but is still energetically active. There is a passage to Hollow Earth from here, leading into a Library within the Great Pyramid of Hollow Earth. This contains the information of the Tibetan origins in Atlantis. Here is stored the information about the White Brotherhood, the secrets of peace and eternal life. The link flows from Hollow Earth, through the Tibetan pyramid to Lakumay, the ascended aspect of Sirius.

~ The Great White Brotherhood ~

In the Golden Era of Atlantis many of the great ascended masters joined their energy together to create The Great White Brotherhood, with the intention of initiating those in incarnation who were pure enough to carry the white light of ascension. White refers to the level of purity they must attain.

Lord Maitreya, Lord of the World, who is responsible for the entire solar system is head of the White Brotherhood and Order of Melchizedek. The Priesthood of Melchizedek, under the direction of Lord Melchizedek, brings illumined mystery teachings to humanity and is part of the Brotherhood. At the Supreme Temple at Heliopolis Jesus prepared for initiation into the Higher Grades of the Great White Brotherhood, after which he became a High Priest in the Order of Melchizedek.

Serapis Bey was a priest avatar in the Ascension Temple in Atlantis and Keeper of the White Flame, the ascension flame. In one of his incarnations he was Akhenaton IV, the Pharoah who protected and re-organized the Great White Brotherhood during his reign and brought back an understanding of one God.

El Morya, who is helping the planet to ascension, is a member of the White brotherhood. He will soon become The Manu, the perfected man, on which the new root race of humanity, with their twelve strands of DNA connected and active, will be based.

Master Lanto, Chohan of the Second Ray, is Master of the Council of the Royal Teton Retreat, which is where the Great White Brother-hood meets in the inner planes.

The Essenes, Cathars, Knights Templar, the Freemasons and the Rosicrucians have spread the teachings of the Great White Brotherhood on Earth in the west. In the East the Sufis, the Chinese Taoists and the Tibetan Lamas pass it on.

The White Brotherhood and the Great White Brotherhood are one and work together for the highest good.

~ Two-way interdimensional portal ~

This pyramid in Tibet is one of four two-way interdimensional portals on the planet. The others are Stonehenge in England, Machu Picchu in Peru, South America and the Great Zimbabwe in Africa.

~ Activating the Key ~

In order to activate the Key to the pyramid in Tibet it helps to work with the unicorns and their energy of purity and perfect peace. The unicorns are seventh-dimensional ascended horses, fully of the angelic realms. They are known as the purest of the pure and their light is enor-mous and shining white. Their third eyes are so evolved that they radi-ate a light from the brow, which appears as a spiralling horn. When you connect with the unicorns it enables every cell in your body to relax and that is the Key to perfect health and eternal life.

~ Babaji ~

An example of eternal life is the great Master Babaji who has lived for thousands of years in a physical body and appears when it is required. He is a great yogi, who uses his yogic powers or Siddhas for the healing or enhancement of humanity. He is a Mahavatar, which means a great avatar. He is known as the deathless avatar because he took the decision to remain on Earth in service to humanity and he shows himself as an eternally young man.

Babaji carries Source energy in a physical body and has always watched over our progress.

I always loved the story of his conversation with his almost equally evolved sister. She asked if he would stay to help humanity and he said, 'It does not matter.' So she said, 'If it does not matter, then stay,' and he agreed he would.

■ **The KEY of the Great Cosmic Pyramid in Tibet is total relaxation, which enables deep, divine, inner peace – the peace that passeth all understanding. The symbol is the pure white dove.**

■ **The SOUND is that of the wings of a dove.**

■ **The COLOUR is brilliant white.**

EXERCISE: *Visualization to carry the White Light*

1. Find a place where you can be quiet and undisturbed.
2. Light a candle if possible to raise the energy.
3. Relax and close your eyes.
4. Ground yourself by imagining your feet growing roots going deep down into the earth.
5. Place Archangel Michael's blue cloak around you.
6. Ask the unicorns to pour their light of enlightenment into your third eye. Feel it coming in.
7. Ask Lord Maitreya to place the pure White Flame over you and sense this happening.
8. Breathe the white light into every cell and relax as deeply as you can.
9. As it spreads through your body feel deep, divine, inner peace filling you.
10. When you are deeply relaxed see a pure white dove flying from you to touch others.
11. Thank the unicorns and Lord Maitreya.
12. Bring your awareness back into the room and open your eyes.

EXERCISE: *To work with the White Flame*

1. Get some crayons and paper and find a place where you can be quiet and undisturbed.
2. Focus on the White Ascension Flame
3. Draw a pyramid.
4. Over it outline the White Flame.
5. Draw a white dove flying from the pyramid.
6. Give yourself time to daydream

The Pyramid under Machu Picchu, Peru

After the fall of Atlantis one of six cosmic pyramids containing the wisdom of Atlantis was built here under the site where Machu Picchu now stands. It is linked to Saturn and the Moon and holds one of the Keys to the universe.

The pyramid has now been destroyed completely but is still energetically active. It is the linking point between Hollow Earth, Saturn and the Moon.

The angels of communication access Earth through this portal bringing symbols that they plant as crop circles where they are needed to expand the minds of humanity.

The Silver Ray, carrying the divine feminine light, also comes through here to Earth and Hollow Earth. This portal is about the power of the divine feminine and the right use of that power. It is about seeing the whole picture and having an objective view.

Machu Picchu is one of the four two-way inter-dimensional portals on Earth. The others are in Tibet, Stonehenge in the UK, and the Great Zimbabwe in Africa and they allow beings to move in and out of the universe.

Commander Ashtar, who is in charge of the intergalactic fleet of spaceships stationed round Earth, is the guardian of the portal of Machu Picchu. He belongs to the Hierarchy of the Great Central Sun and his vast fleet of spaceships patrol this universe. They are particularly engaged in protecting our planet and us.

He and his fleet connect to Earth and also access Hollow Earth through this place. This is the only portal through which he can bring his mothership, which is an enormous energy almost as large as Lady Gaia herself. He only has one mother ship and once through the portal it moves to places where its huge energy can be accepted. These are New

Zealand, Avebury in the West Country of England, Uluru in Australia, Guatemala in South America, The Himalayas, Mount Shasta in the US and the Hollow Earth Portal in the US.

The mothership visits Avebury in the west country of England which used to be the welcome portal for spaceships from the universes and is now being reenergized to work in this way again. Some of the crop circles planted in this area are coded messages reminding us to connect with the wisdom of the extraterrestrials.

Uluru in Australia is also a place where its energy can be received and this area is being prepared to accept more spacecrafts in the near future. The Australians will listen to the wisdom and technological guidance of those from other stars and planets and this will help the entire world in due course.

Guatemala, South America, the location of the cosmic heart, is very open to the higher energy of the space visitors who wish to share their knowledge with us on Earth. After the fall of Atlantis the three tribes who originated from Venus, the planet of love, settled in South America. These were the Incas, the Aztecs and the Mayans. Eventually they spread their loving influence across the continent. Guatemala will welcome the wisdom and love of the extraterrestrials, who will help this country to become a blazing light for the planet.

The Himalayas is a very pure and ancient place, which can easily accept the light of this vast spacecraft.

Mount Shasta in the mountains of Northern California is also a very pure portal, where spacecrafts are often seen and Commander Ashtar brings his mothership here where it radiates light into the surrounding areas.

Hollow Earth is one of the cosmic portals in the US, which will start to open in 2012. It covers North Dakota, South Dakota, Nebraska, Kansas and Oklahoma. There is much ancient spiritual energy held in the land here, which allows the energy of the mothercraft to be accepted here.

New Zealand is a spaceship zone. While I was on holiday there I saw several small spaceships, then I had the unforgettable experience of glimpsing Commander Ashtar's mothership just for a moment. It was like the most enormous liner with all its portholes ablaze with light. It was unbelievably vast and I felt very privileged to see it, even though I was not with like-minded people and could not mention it!

At the time when the energy on Earth was beautiful and pure Commander Ashtar would open the portal of Machu Picchu wide so that the angels and beings from other planets and universes could look through it onto us. Now this rarely happens as Ashtar keeps the portal closed much of the time. He opens it only to allow in beings who can benefit the planet.

I was once in Ireland visiting a stone circle. I sat on a stone for a few minutes when suddenly I was aware of Commander Ashtar, dressed in a silver spacesuit in the centre of the circle. He held out a hand and said, 'Come!' I went! I was out of my body and gone. My friends saw that my spirit had gone somewhere and went back to the cars without me! When Commander Ashtar brought me back I had no conscious memory of where he had taken me.

On another occasion I sat down to meditate and Commander Ashtar came in. He placed his hand on my crown and I teleported with him to a spaceship that he piloted himself. He asked me if I would like to visit his mothership. I was thrilled. The mothership was even bigger than I imagined. It was like a huge office block inside with a sense of order and discipline but full of golden light and a feeling of love. He told me we were going through the portal of Machu Picchu into the universe and with a burst of energy we left the planet. All I had was a sense of freedom and wonder and then it was time to come back.

■ **The KEY of the Pyramid under Machu Picchu, Peru, is to trust your intuition and use it wisely and strongly for the highest good.**

■ **The SOUND is the shriek of the condor.**

■ **The COLOUR is silver moonstone.**

The symbol of this portal in Machu Picchu is the six-pointed star within a circle. The six-pointed star consists of two triangles, one pointing up and the other down. Together they symbolize the bringing of Earth to Heaven and Heaven to Earth. This is one of the most profound and ancient spiritual symbols.

Note that the Key to the knowledge held by Ra and the Egyptian tribes is the six-pointed star, while it is the symbol of Machu Picchu.

EXERCISE: *Visualization to journey with Commander Ashtar*

1. Find a place where you can be quiet and undisturbed.
2. Light a candle if possible to raise the energy.
3. Relax and close your eyes.
4. Ground yourself by imagining roots going from you deep into the earth.
5. Place Archangel Michael's blue cloak for protection around you.
6. Place the six-pointed star in a circle over each of your chakras in turn, the Stellar Gateway, the Soul Star, the causal, the crown, the third eye, the throat, the heart, the solar plexus, the navel, the sacral, the base and the Earth Star.
7. Ask Commander Ashtar to visit you and sense when his energy touches you.
8. Follow him into his spacecraft and let him take you on a journey through the portal of Machu Picchu into the universe.
9. Where do you go? What do you experience? How does your journey serve?
10. What is your interaction with Commander Ashtar?
11. Ask him for guidance about your spiritual development and how you can serve.
12. Let him bring you back to your starting point when it is time.
13. Then bring your awareness back to your present reality and open your eyes.

EXERCISE: *To follow your gut feelings and intuition*

– Be very aware of your gut feelings and your intuition today.
   Listen to its messages to you and trust it to guide you.
   For example, hear what people say and discern whether it is true for you. Then make your own decisions. Or tune into the food you eat today and let your intuition tell you whether it is right for you. Then choose wisely.

Hollow Earth Portal

As discussed earlier Hollow Earth is a seventh-dimensional paradise in the centre of Earth, which is the true divine blueprint for our planet.

Our spiritual level on Earth has only recently risen to one where we can access the light of Hollow Earth. This means that for the first time the entry portals are meaningful to us.

The Hollow Earth cosmic portal that covers North and South Dakota, Nebraska, Kansas and Oklahoma is linked to Source via the Pleiades. It is also connected to the higher aspects of Sirius. The earth shifts in this portal to bring it back to its correct size and shape will be eased by extraordinary energies that have been planted there in the past in preparation for 2012. For example, in Nebraska in 2012 a deep red-pink energy will start to spread across the whole world from the heart of this state, encouraging people to be kind, calm and nice to each other. This was placed here aeons ago by beings from Venus in preparation for the transition to the Golden Age on Earth. This beautiful light will dissolve karma and totally transform old attitudes.

In addition wise beings came to Oklahoma a very long time ago. They brought great knowledge and love, which has been stored within the land to be released in 2012.

In South Dakota, when the portal opens Seraphim with their extraordinary high frequency will touch and physically affect people's heart chakras. Many will experience illumination and great happiness.

These energies will bring inner peace to the people living there and they will then be able to link into the wisdom of the Native Americans and fully honour the Earth again. People will tune into the divine blueprint for the planet and this will prompt a desire within them to follow the divine will.

~ Portals into Hollow Earth ~

When angels and masters have entered Hollow Earth through this portal they can feel exactly what Earth is feeling and know what is happening to the planet and everyone on it.

They can send high-frequency energy along the ley lines to clear them and this may cause an earthquake if there is a blockage.

An example of this is the earthquake in Haiti, where the blockage was caused by black magic and fear of it over the centuries. This event has shaken people up to think and act differently. It has also resulted in a huge heart-opening for humanity. However, this natural disaster could have been countered if enough people had sent the Gold Ray of Christ to dissolve the stuck energy. Please continue to send the healing, love, wisdom and protection of the Gold Ray of Christ to this place and any others that you sense needs clearance.

See the Orbs of the Archangels Metatron, Uriel and an angel of love below, also an Orb of Archangel Chamuel with Mother Mary and an angel of love on page 110.

■ **The KEY of the Hollow Earth portal is to have inner peace and follow the divine will.**

■ **The SOUND is that of innocent laughter.**

■ **The COLOUR is rainbow.**

The Archangels Metatron, Uriel and an angel of love. This Orb illuminates you to aspire to a higher way of being by opening you up to Source.

Photograph by Jeff Archer

EXERCISE: *Visualization to heal the area around the Hollow Earth Portal*

1. Find a place where you can be quiet and undisturbed.
2. Light a candle if possible to raise the energy.
3. Relax and close your eyes.
4. Ground yourself by imagining roots going from you deep into the earth.
5. Place Archangel Michael's blue cloak around you.
6. Visualize the gold and silver violet flame in a six-pointed star over the Hollow Earth portal.
7. See the flame transmuting all lower energies into beautiful light.
8. Imagine the people and animals happy, the trees and waters radiant and pure.
9. When you have finished, consciously detach from any lower energy you may have picked up and see yourself as cleansed and pure as well.
10. Then bring your awareness back into the room and open your eyes.

EXERCISE: *To draw the gold and silver violet flame in a star*

– Draw a gold and silver violet six-pointed star and place it on a map over North and South Dakota, Oklahoma, Kansas and Nebraska to transmute old energy and raise the frequency of the area. You may like to place it in other places on your map that you feel need cleansing.

EXERCISE: *Visualization to develop the qualities of Golden Earth*

– This will help you to start feeling the heartbeat of the planet. When you enter Hollow Earth through this portal you really connect with the blueprint of the planet and start to see your role in the changes ahead more clearly.

1. Find a place where you can be quiet and undisturbed.
2. Light a candle if possible.
3. Relax and close your eyes.
4. Ground yourself by imagining roots going from you deep into the earth.

5. Place Archangel Michael's protective blue cloak around you.
6. Focus in the fifth-dimension on the area of this portal.
   Send love and peace here and visualize it being green, fertile,
   rich in bird life and all the animals well treated and contented.
7. Take yourself above the portal and look down at it.
8. Breathe in the higher light you sense rising from here.
9. Feel your heart expand with love.
10. Return to the place where you started and open your eyes.

Honolulu

The portal of Honolulu brings higher love and via this, Lady Gaia is now spreading agape from Venus through Earth into Hollow Earth and into the planet. The cosmic portal at Honolulu is the sacral chakra of the planet in the charge of Archangel Gabriel who is also in charge of the navel chakra near Fuji. His retreat is the portal of Mount Shasta. He is working to purify our understanding of sexuality and raise it to a transcendent level. As agape spreads and masculine and feminine energies on the planet come into balance, the higher frequency will enable true love and higher sexual expression to blossom and flower.

The energy from this portal is already starting to help teenagers to handle their feelings in such a way that they can make decisions about their sexuality in a wiser way than acting from lust or rose-tinted love. It will enable them to feel balanced and learn about respectful love for others and themselves. This will impact very positively on the children of the future who will feel safer in the love of their parents.

The love coming through this portal will also help people to use unconditional love to dissolve karma from past relationships. The moment we free the cords of the past, we invite higher quality relationships into our lives, new doors open bringing in wider possibilities, healings take place as emotional blocks release and we can find our own happiness. The quality of all our relationships will deepen and grow.

Agape enables individuals within families to remain free yet connected. Many family groups have been like skeins of wool, emotionally entangled and involved, so that the individuals cannot be themselves and yet they cannot escape. In other cases members move as far away as possible because they feel trapped when they are near their relatives. As higher love flows in through this portal more individuals will be able to be themselves, express themselves honestly, do what is right for their own lives, follow their hearts – and at the same time feel connected to their family. For the first time for thousands of years family dynamics will become rich and supportive, because people will be linked by higher love.

Tune into the beautiful vibration of the Orb of an angel of love with Mother Mary and Archangel Chamuel below.

■ **The KEY of Honolulu is to develop and practise agape or higher love.**

■ **The SOUND is that of angels singing about love.**

■ **The COLOUR is rose pink.**

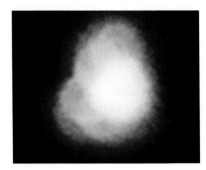

Angel of Love with Mother Mary and Archangel Chamuel. When you look at this Orb it holds you in deep loving assurance, so that you know you are loved.

Photograph by Diana Cooper

EXERCISE: *Visualization to enable love to blossom*

1. Find a place where you can be quiet and undisturbed.
2. If possible, light a candle to raise the vibration.
3. Relax and close your eyes.
4. Ground yourself by imagining roots growing from the soles of your feet deep into the earth.
5. Place Archangel Michael's blue cloak around you for protection.
6. Imagine you are over the portal in Honolulu and are breathing higher love into your sacral chakra.
7. Picture your entire extended family together and see the higher love dissolving all cords and lower emotions.
8. See yourself with your friends, business colleagues and acquaintances. Feel the higher love sweeping like a gentle tide through you, washing away all lower feelings.
9. See all the sexual links you have ever had being purified by agape from Venus.

10. When you feel relaxed and full of love, let Archangel Gabriel place a pure white cloak of light and higher love round you. Absorb its energy and know that whenever you need to in the future you can breathe in the pure love.

11. Bring yourself back to where you started from, open your eyes and look at all your relationships with new eyes of love.

EXERCISE: *To clear your sacral chakra*

For this you will need some wool or string, scissors, blu-tack or plasticine and a pink flower or drawing of one.

1. In the sacral chakra we hold sexual and emotional blocks. Decide who you want to release from your sacral chakra.

2. Stick your blu-tack or plasticine, representing your sacral chakra, onto a hard surface. Thick cardboard will do.

3. For each person you intend to release cut a length of wool or string and attach it to the plasticine.

4. Send love to each of the people you are releasing.

5. Then ask Archangel Gabriel to help you gently loosen those cords from your chakra with love, taking the woollen strings out of your plasticine.

6. When you have done so, bury the cords in the earth with respect and ask Gaia to transform them into beautiful flowers. The most important thing here is to put energy and intention into this action.

The Dogon Portal,
Mali, Africa

At the fall of Atlantis, the Egyptian tribe under the leadership of the High Priest Ra, came to Africa. Part of that tribe, the Dogons, moved down the continent to Mali. The Dogons hold and have always held the higher wisdom of Lakumay, Sirius. Not only do they maintain the memory of the movement of many stars including Sirius but also their dances reveal the sacred geometry that we need to heal the world.

When you connect to Hollow Earth through this portal you feel the beat and rhythm of Sirius and other stars, planets and constellations and it is through this energetic link that they download their wisdom to you. This is how the Dogons keep the connection. It may help you to read about them and discover more of their understandings.

If you look at Sirius on a map or go outside and see it in the sky, then really tune in and listen, you will make a connection to its wisdom.

You can also link to the higher wisdom of Lakumay, Sirius through sacred geometry: triangles, circles, squares, ovals, stars, the infinity sign and pyramids, tetrahedrons, spheres or cubes.

The animals that originate from Sirius, or its ascended aspect Lakumay, which is currently invisible to us, also carry some of the wisdom of this star. Cows, nurturing, loving, stable and solid and their masculine counterpart, the bull, demonstrating power and protective energy descended from Lakumay. So do horses that show such love, dignity and self-worth. Deer too came from here. See Key 31 for information about which birds come from Sirius and which from Lakumay. Dolphins brought their wisdom and cosmic knowledge from Lakumay and people used to telepathically tune in to them and download it.

Dogs, the beloved friends and companions of humans, come from the constellation of Canis Major, in which the brightest star is Sirius, often called the Dog Star.

Many of the beings of Sirius have highly developed minds and carry knowledge of advanced technology and science, which they are teaching to us. In his lifetime as Pythagoras, Lord Kuthumi the World Teacher, brought through much information and knowledge from this star. The Master Hilarion, Chohan of the Fifth Ray of Science and Technology, spreads information about technology and sacred geometry. We were once sent a wonderful photograph of him in an Orb bringing students to watch a spider weaving its web using sacred geometry.

■ **The KEY of the Dogon Portal in Mali is to bring in the wisdom of Sirius through sacred geometry.**

■ **The SOUND is that of dancing with bare feet on soft earth.**

■ **The COLOUR is royal blue.**

EXERCISE: *Visualization to access cosmic wisdom*

1. Find a place where you can be quiet and undisturbed.
2. Light a candle if possible.
3. Relax and close your eyes.
4. Ground yourself by growing imaginary roots from your feet deep into the earth.
5. Place Archangel Michael's blue protective cloak around you.
6. Visualize Master Hilarion, the Master of the Fifth Ray of Science and Technology, appearing in front of you, surrounded by orange light.
7. He is linking you via silver triangles to a dolphin and to Sirius; then to the Dogons and Sirius; then to Hollow Earth and Sirius.
8. You may feel the lines of the triangles vibrating as energy is passed to you.
9. Relax and absorb whatever is right for you.
10. Thank Master Hilarion, the dolphin, the Dogons as well as Hollow Earth and Sirius and know you are being opened up.
11. Return to the place where you started, bring your awareness back to the room and open your eyes.

EXERCISE: *To connect to the wisdom of Sirius*

1. Look at a map on which Sirius is marked or even better go outside and find it in the night sky.
2. Relax and think about the Dogon portal into Hollow Earth from the higher aspect of Sirius.
3. As you do this make a pattern of geometrical shapes, triangles, circles, squares, ovals, stars and the infinity sign and pyramids, tetrahedrons, spheres or cubes.
4. Stay open to information being downloaded to you as you doodle.

The Bermuda Triangle

The Great Crystal of Atlantis was made from pure Source energy and programmed with the wisdom of that civilization and their connection to the stars. It was housed in the temple of Poseidon, which collapsed at the fall of Atlantis; thus the Great Crystal descended to the bottom of the ocean in the centre of the Bermuda Triangle. Because, amongst other things, the crystal was a portal it continued to act as such from the bottom of the sea. This is an inter-dimensional portal that has been available to us for the past ten thousand years.

The information encoded and stored within the Great Crystal becomes available whenever the portal here opens. At one time it rarely did so, partly because the consequences were so dramatic for anyone who was in the triangle at the time. With the agreement of their souls they went through a rapid change of frequency and ascended to a different level.

Now the portal is being utilized more frequently but the effect of the opening is less severe because the frequency of the planet has risen and the energies can be managed more readily.

When you are asleep at night your spirit leaves your physical sheath, the body, and travels to different places on the inner planes. If you are aligned with Golden Atlantis you may find that your spirit often goes to this portal without you being consciously aware of it, to be taught about the wisdom of that time and to retrieve your former gifts and talents. You can also specifically direct your spirit to go to a specific location in the inner planes. Now that more people are realizing this they are asking to visit the Great Crystal in the Bermuda Triangle during their sleep.

The Bermuda Triangle is connected to Neptune, one of the four ascension planets working symbiotically with Earth. Until 2009 the wisdom from both Lemuria and Atlantis held on Neptune was blocked to us. It has now been freed so we can access all the wisdom held in the Great Crystal of Atlantis via this portal. It holds all the spiritual technology that awaits us when we fully raise our frequency to the fifth dimension. We can work with Master Hilarion, Chohan of the Fifth Ray of science and technology, to help us bring this forward now.

■ **The KEY of the Bermuda Triangle is to tune into the Great Crystal of Atlantis with expectation.**

■ **The SOUND is the murmur of a rippling sea.**

■ **The COLOUR is sea-green.**

EXERCISE: *Visualization to contact the Great Crystal of Atlantis with a Dolphin*

1. Find a place where you are undisturbed and can be still.
2. Light a candle if possible.
3. Relax and close your eyes.
4. Ground yourself by imagining roots going from you deep into the earth.
5. Place Archangel Michael's blue cloak around you.
6. See a beautiful warm and welcoming, clear sea-green ocean in front of you.
7. A dolphin is approaching you, full of fun, joy and wisdom.
8. He assures you that you are totally safe with him and lets you ride on his back through the waves.
9. Knowing that you are protected and secure, go with the dolphin's flow as he takes you down into the depths. In the inner planes you can breathe quite easily and freely.
10. Ahead you can see the high-frequency light of the Bermuda Triangle. You may feel a change of energy as you enter it.
11. The dolphin now takes you to the Great Crystal. As you touch it, you feel a sensation of anticipation.
12. Connect with the wisdom within the Great Crystal. Take your time to experience it and let anything you need to know percolate into your being.
13. Now your dolphin is nudging you and suggesting it is time to return.
14. Once more be aware of the sea-green of the waters as you move graciously with your dolphin back to the place where you started.
15. Open your eyes and write down what you experienced.

EXERCISE: *To visit the Bermuda Triangle portal and the Great Crystal of Atlantis during sleep*

1. During the day think or read about the Bermuda Triangle and the Great Crystal of Atlantis.
2. Before you go to sleep relax your physical body.
3. Ground yourself by imagining roots going from your body deep into the earth.
4. Place Archangel Michael's blue cloak of protection around yourself.
5. Invoke the Universal Angel Joules who is in charge of the Oceans and whose etheric retreat is at the Bermuda Triangle.
6. When you have a sense of his presence ask permission to visit his retreat to learn about the wisdom of Atlantis and to retrieve your ancient wisdom.
7. You may receive a direct invitation or have a feeling that you are granted permission.
8. Then direct your spirit to go there. You do this by affirming clearly that you will be visiting the Bermuda Triangle.
9. As you wait to go to sleep breathe comfortably and think about the wonder of Golden Atlantis.

Some people find it easier to access energy or information when they are drawing or doodling. Let your mind wander freely as you do this.

EXERCISE: *To connect with the Bermuda Triangle portal and the Great Crystal of Atlantis*

1. Find paper and some coloured pens.
2. First draw the Bermuda Triangle in any form, real or symbolic that you wish to.
3. Draw a crystal to represent the Great Crystal.
4. Choose a sea-green if possible to represent the ocean and colour it in.
5. You may like to fill in sea creatures, a dolphin, a treasure chest of wisdom, the Universal Angel Joules or any angel or being that you intuitively feel is important.
6. When you have finished you may find an issue or problem is clearer to you or that you have accessed something you did not know before, or that you feel you would like to visit the portal in your sleep!

The Ocean near Fiji

Alcyon is the brightest star in the cluster of the Pleiades, which is one of the four ascension stars, planets or constellations connected with Earth. The beings from here radiate blue healing energy. From Alcyon high-frequency energy flows to Earth into the portal located in the ocean near Fiji. This facilitates the cleansing and natural growth of our planet, enabling the frequency to rise.

This healing light is coming through Fiji, which is the spiritual navel centre of Earth, in order to bring more friendship, warmth, togetherness and co-operation to humanity. Archangel Gabriel is in charge of this portal and is helping to spread the energy from here to other parts of the world to touch the people, cleanse the planet and raise it into the fifth dimension.

When the healing flows through the portal of Fiji into Hollow Earth, these higher qualities affect the blueprint of Earth. Then Lady Gaia can send the changes out to the planet and they touch every creature.

As we practise openness, warmth, friendship, co-operation, harmony, being welcoming and togetherness our fifth-dimensional navel chakra opens and our lives will be transformed. True community will automatically flourish. As this continues to happen we will become open and welcoming towards high-frequency beings from other planets who are waiting to help us.

■ **The KEY of the ocean near Fiji is to practise friendship, warmth, togetherness and co-operation to promote harmony at a fifth-dimensional level.**

■ **The SOUND is that of celebration.**

■ **The COLOUR is orange.**

EXERCISE: *Visualization to connect to your navel chakra*

1. Find a place where you can be quiet and undisturbed.
2. Light a candle if possible.
3. Relax and close your eyes.
4. Ground yourself by imagining roots going from you deep into the earth.
5. Place Archangel Michael's blue protective cloak around you.
6. Breathe beautiful warm, welcoming orange light into your navel chakra.
7. Visualize yourself transported to the glorious, white sand of the island of Fiji.
8. Be aware of the rustle of the palm leaves and the lapping of the waves.
9. There are many strangers, laughing and chatting.
10. Feeling warm, relaxed, confident and open, go up to them and laugh with them.
11. You are all holding hands dancing and stamping.
12. Feel you are totally accepted as one of them, welcome and belonging.
13. Now take yourself somewhere else into a difficult situation with this chakra open. You are radiating warm, welcoming energy.
14. Approach the people you meet in this new place openly and lovingly. Transform the energy so that you are all co-operating and enjoying each other's company.
15. When you have felt the power of this chakra open and operating at a fifth-dimensional level, return to where you started.
16. Open your eyes and remember the powerful vibration of this chakra.

EXERCISE: *To connect to Fiji*

1. Find a shell.
2. Hold it to your ear and imagine that it is connected to the shells of Fiji.
3. Listen to the sounds of the ocean and know you are receiving a connection to this portal.

EXERCISE: *Co-operation and welcome*

- Open your sacral chakra and then work in co-operation with some-one today.
- Be friendly and welcoming to acquaintances and strangers and notice what happens and how you feel.

The Bird Kingdom

All birds originate from Sirius. Some come from its ascended aspect, Lakumay, and use Sirius to step-down their frequency. Birds belong to a group soul. When their particular group of about a hundred ascends to Lakumay, they become individualized.

Birds have many of the qualities of angels and they incarnated to demonstrate that it is possible to fly with your heart open and yet have a physical body. Like the angels, birds demonstrate qualities of light such as joy, freedom, caring and living in the moment.

Songbirds sing from their hearts whatever the conditions. They share with us the pure messages of the angels through their song but we have not yet learnt to hear them. They might sing the same tune but every time they do so, it carries a different communication. The Key is in the song but the plethora of qualities they come in to teach is part of that.

Various breeds of birds also come to teach diverse things. They do not come to Earth to learn.

Most birds show us their incredible qualities of patience as they wait for food to come to them. They fly so fast and close together but their advanced sonar ensures that they never collide.

~ Albatross ~

The albatross in the bird kingdom is like the lion in the animal kingdom. It demonstrates its majesty by being totally at peace with itself. Its serenity and oneness with the elements is its power and this is what it teaches us. The albatross comes from Lakumay.

~ Eagle, condor, hawk ~

Eagles and condors are from Lakumay but not hawks, which are less evolved and are still part of a group soul. Eagles and condors are Masters of Air, they have mastered their element. They demonstrate far sight and vision as they gracefully soar on the currents. They teach us that when you are a master life flows easily and naturally.

They also teach transformational transition. Their sound is a shout, which indicates screaming out the old so that the new can come in at a higher level.

~ Gulls ~

When we see gulls quarrelling, bullying or stealing food from smaller birds we see a mirror of our own disharmony. Then they fly and glide on the currents of air, showing us a higher aspect of themselves and our souls.

~ Humming Birds ~

However many times we see a humming bird, we cannot help gasping at their brilliant colours, their balance and serenity. They carry the wisdom of Lemuria and pass it on through their presence. Humming birds come from Lakumay.

~ Ostrich, emu, cassowary ~

These are flightless birds that have adapted to be fast runners and they show us that if you cannot do things one way, there is another. They demonstrate qualities of sociability with each other, protectiveness and curiosity.

~ Parrot family – budgerigars, cockatoo ~

This family of vibrantly coloured birds is very advanced, using tools and mimicking words and sounds of humans and other animals. They have developed and fine-tuned the quality of listening to a high degree. The parrot family come from Lakumay.

~ Peacocks ~

They demonstrate the difference between the sexes. In this particular instance the male is happy and proud of his appearance. He is flamboyant, visible and egotistical, his shrill cry indicating a lack of harmony.

His actions and attitude protects the quiet, dully coloured female who can then safely carry out the role of motherhood. They teach us to look beyond the outer show.

~ Penguin, puffin ~

Penguins are showing us something special. They are flightless and coloured black and white, the colours of the Earth Star chakra, because they are grounded – though other black and white creatures are not necessarily demonstrating a connection to Earth. Archangel Sandalphon who is in charge of the Earth Star Chakra appears as grey, which is a merging of the black and white, masculine and feminine. Penguins balance these opposites too. Both male and female care for their eggs and their young chicks equally. They show a high level of courage, protection, discipline and devotion. Penguins connect to Hollow Earth through the Earth Star chakra.

Puffins on the other hand are softer and more feminine. They show a wonderful sense of freedom within responsibility. They teach us that it is possible to be connected to the planet through water and earth but the puffins connect to Hollow Earth through the Universal Angel Joules whose etheric retreat is within the Bermuda Triangle.

They teach us that you can make your connections in different ways as long as you do it with joy and a sense of freedom.

Both breeds of birds come from Lakumay.

~ Vulture ~

These scavengers show us that it is important to clean up our environment. Everyone and everything has a place in nature; nothing needs to be wasted.

~ Swans ~

When a cygnet is young it is brown. As it grows into adulthood it develops pure white feathers signifying it is pure and regal. Black swans are the yin to the white of the other birds and that also indicates a majestic quality. All swans carry grace, acceptance and serenity. They come from Lakumay.

~ Hedgerow birds – sparrow, thrush, blackbird,
tit, robin, cuckoo, lark, warbler ~

These much-appreciated little songbirds demonstrate domestic love in all its variations. They sing to us daily the messages of the angels and help to keep us informed and in tune with the cosmic energies. It is time to replace the hedges so that they can continue their wonderful work.

~ Migratory birds – swallow, swift,
most geese, martins ~

These birds show us that more can be accomplished when we do things together than when we act alone. They work in total harmony, taking it in turns to lead, without having a nominated leader. This is a gift they developed in the time of Lemuria. These birds are healers, who send out a healing energy to all of nature. When they fly over the land they link into the ley lines and their sonic lights them up, raising their frequency.

~ Grouse, pheasant, moorhen, coot, duck,
partridge, dove, pigeon, plover ~

They peck the ground and help to prepare it for seeds to grow. The water birds pull on the weeds to the same effect. They are all carrying the message of love and peace from the angels and often they try to come physically close to humans to convey this message. As we humans raise our frequency and feel more at peace with ourselves we will return love to these birds and welcome them into our lives.

~ Hens ~

Chickens come from a distant asteroid and step down through Sirius. They have come to offer us feathers and eggs and to teach humans that it is good to serve.

~ Owls ~

Owls bring their energy down from Lakumay. They bring with them wisdom and vision. They work with the elementals at night offering them teaching and protection. They clear unwanted energies in the areas where they live. They hold the vision for the fifth-dimensional planet and try to draw the attention of people to what needs to be done.

~ Pelicans ~

These dinosaur-like birds incarnated in the time of Mu, the civilization before Lemuria. They remind us of the past and of the fact that Earth has been developing for a very long time. They hold the collective memories from Mu that we are allowed to access and show us how to accept things as they are.

~ Kingfisher, heron, crane, ibis ~

They show us how to wait patiently with positive intention, focus on our goal and then go for it. They teach us the power of pure thinking.

~ Magpie, crow, rook, raven ~

Like vultures these birds eat carrion and help all of nature to be usefully used. More importantly they all work with Archangel Azriel, the angel of death and birth, as his messengers both in the animal and human kingdom. If a baby animal is about to be born one of these birds will arrive to warn the mother to prepare herself.

The ancients recognized this but called it a superstition. They say if you see one of these birds alone there will be sorrow. In fact they are telling you that you have created a karmic challenge and must raise your vibration. Therefore they are messengers of enlightenment. It may simply be that you have had a lower thought and need to speak and act differently.

~ Wading birds – flamingo, oystercatcher ~

Water is the glue of the universe and connects all things with love. Spending their time in this medium keeps these wading birds pure and reminds us of the healing, cosmic properties of water. As a result these birds see through the outer into the essence of the inner. They work harmoniously with the elements to reach fulfilment. Their message is to keep life simple and go with the flow.

■ **The KEY of the bird kingdom is to take in the qualities that the birds teach us through the vibration of the sounds they make.**

■ **The SOUND is the singing of the dawn chorus.**

■ **The COLOUR is the azure blue of a clear sky.**

EXERCISE: *Visualization to listen to the message of a bird*

1. Find a place where you can be quiet and undisturbed.
2. Light a candle if possible, to raise the vibration.
3. Relax and close your eyes.
4. Ground yourself by imagining roots going from you deep into the earth.
5. Place Archangel Michael's blue cloak of protection around you.
6. Picture yourself in a beautiful place out in nature. You may find yourself in your homeland or somewhere abroad.
7. As you sit quietly watch a bird flying. It approaches you and lands quite close to you.
8. This bird has a message for you. Listen with your heart.
9. Thank the bird for coming to you and watch it move away.
10. Return to your waking reality and open your eyes.

EXERCISE: *To connect with the bird kingdom*

1. Take time to walk outside.
2. Watch and listen to the birds.
3. Note which birds come to you and the messages they carry for you.

The Animal Kingdom

Every animal has a soul or is part of a group soul and is on its own journey to ascension. They come to Earth to experience, learn and teach, just as we do.

Different animals come from all over the universes. Some are highly evolved and maintain a fifth-dimensional energy while on this planet. Others are third-dimensional. Most take their experiences back to their home planets to enrich them.

Once on Earth the way we treat the animals affects their incarnations and their spiritual growth.

All animals work with the Universal Angel Fhelyai to bring an understanding of the Animal Kingdom to Earth and spread their messages to every sentient being on the planet.

THE PLEIADES

The Pleiades star cluster is often known as the seven sisters and it radiates feminine light and wonderful blue healing energy. Their healing is based on wholeness and truth. Beings from the Pleiades are bringing healing to people and places on Earth.

~ Pandas ~

Pandas heal by their presence and by being loving and in balance. They also actively send healing and connect people to the Pleiades and to the angels of the Pleiades. They have chosen to be black and white to show people that not everything is one extreme or the other and to see with eyes of love. Pandas hold strong inner peace and their hearts are innocent and pure. Their qualities arouse compassion, empathy and love in people and open their hearts. This is why children love pandas as cuddly toys.

Mother Mary works with pandas and helps to connect them to the cosmic heart. Through the animals she also helps to link people to the cosmic heart.

~ Pigs ~

These bright, intelligent animals were very respected and loved when they first came to Earth. They help the ecological balance by eating waste food and they radiate healing, wisdom and peace to people and the land where they live. Where friendship is offered they accept it gladly and return it multiplied.

ORION

Orion is known as the planet of enlightenment, where there are many established training schools for those spirits who are ready to accept cosmic wisdom. Beings from here have very fast-frequency energy in their auras and open others to their special light.

~ Bears ~

These magnificent animals are demonstrating the right use of power and authority when they are in the natural habitat for their species.

~ Cats ~

All cats whether small domestic ones or huge lions and tigers bring qualities of enlightenment to Earth. They are independent beings, re-laxed when it is appropriate to be so, and they do not need humans. They are very psychic and know exactly what is happening at all times. Domestic cats have accepted responsibility for keeping the homes of their 'owners' clear of lower energies. The big cats watch over our planet and protect it from unwanted entities. They are also healers.

~ Giraffes ~

These wise animals show qualities of gentleness, dignity and grace. Al-though they seem to have more feminine characteristics they are very well balanced and able to protect themselves when necessary. They help trees by trimming and thinning their top leaves.

~ Goats ~

Goats bring higher energy and enlightenment to the world. They have qualities of healing, generous giving, wisdom and humility. They also help with the ecology and waste disposal.

~ Hedgehogs ~

Everyone loves hedgehogs because they sense their harmlessness and high-frequency qualities. Despite their prickles they promote wisdom by bringing laughter, relaxation and joy to people.

~ Red Squirrels ~

These delightful high-frequency enlightened beings demonstrate joy, vitality, freedom and happiness. They show us how to live lightly and have fun. Grey squirrels are from Sirius.

~ Rabbits ~

Rabbits demonstrate qualities of caring, nurturing, softness and fun. They are healers of the heart, which they do with wisdom and love. They work with the Universal Angel Gabriel to spread purity and joy.

Part of the wisdom they bring to us is to remind us to connect to the song of the Earth. They listen and hear when a predator or a human is approaching because its vibrations change the song of the Earth. This ability is also their protection.

SIRIUS and its ascended aspect LAKUMAY

Sirius in the constellation Canis Major, the Greater Dog, is the brightest star in the night sky. It is known as the star of Isis. The Dogons of Africa are from Lakumay. They hold the wisdom of Sirius and dance its movements. Sirius holds spiritual technology and sacred geometry for the universe and downloads it to those who are ready to visit its training establishments in the inner planes. Here the Ascended Master Hilarion works with them. The children being born who incarnate from or through Sirius are programmed with the new higher technology for use in the New Golden Age.

~ Cows ~

Cows come from Lakumay. They originally came to offer us milk, which in the times of Golden Atlantis was in perfect alignment with the vibrations of humans. They show a great capacity for giving and are solid, reliable and steady. The cow is loving and nurturing, the bull powerful and protective. Between them they demonstrate a perfect masculine and feminine balance.

While their oversoul has been exploring the possibility of withdrawing from Earth to further their experience on another planet, now that the frequency of this one is beginning to rise they will remain here. They will enjoy sharing their gifts and furthering their growth in the fifth dimension.

~ Horses ~

Like cows horses originate from Lakumay, the ascended aspect of Sirius. In the beginning they were ridden bareback and directed telepathically by their riders. They were free creatures, who generously gave us their energy to help us. They are highly evolved beings here to learn and teach about love, dignity and self-worth. They are healers, who raise the frequency of those in need with their presence.

~ Deer ~

The deer and stag between them balance the masculine and feminine energies. The stag is dignified, strong, proud and courageous while the deer is gentle, loving and in harmony. They are learning and teaching about trust.

~ Camels and dromedaries ~

Camels and dromedaries both originate from Lakumay and are very wise, intelligent creatures. They are learning and teaching about service with patience and endurance and also bring our focus to using resources wisely. As soon as the people in their parts of the world have raised their frequencies these animals will telepathically impart their wisdom to them in order to help them come more easily through the transition period from 2012 to 2032.

~ Elephants ~

These huge gentle creatures originate from Lakumay to learn and teach about family life and structure while in a physical body. They are dignified, strong, caring and intuitive, while clearly demonstrating majesty and presence. At the same time they enjoy innocent joyous fun.

~ Dogs ~

Known as the Dog Star, Sirius is one of the stars of the constellation of Canis Major. Dogs, wolves, foxes, coyote and hyenas have all originated from here.

Wolves teach about society structure, discipline, dignity, endurance and many higher qualities including love. Domestic dogs show us pure unconditional love and how to be a faithful companion and friend, yet still maintain their original essence or blueprint.

Kathy has had two ectopic miscarriages. She knew she had a girl and boy in spirit, but she had never connected to them. One evening her dog Jake suddenly stood on his back legs and started to bark loudly at the ceiling. He immediately understood that her children had come to see her and was alerting her to it. As soon as Kathy realized what was going on, he relaxed and went back to his snooze.

MARS and its ascended aspect NIGELLAY

Mars is known as the red planet because of the colour of its rock. Metaphysically red represents energy, which can turn to aggression and Mars has been a warlike planet, whose beings were the warriors defending our universe. However, its ascended aspect Nigellay embodies the qualities of the peaceful warrior and this is what the training schools in the inner planes of Mars are instilling into those who visit here.

~ Kangaroos and Wallabies ~

Kangaroos and wallabies have the qualities of the peaceful warrior. They tread lightly on the land. They are gentle and nurturing of their vulnerable young, yet they empower them by giving them freedom to learn while being protected.

They demonstrate the right use of kundalini, bounding and so being light on the land.

They originally incarnated at the same time as the Aborigines and have a strong telepathic communication with them. They bring in Lemurian energy. Wherever they go they are healing the land and sending Lemurian healing down the ley lines.

When they are in the right environment and everything around them is in harmony, they are in tune with the flow of nature, the wind, the earth and the plants. Then they demonstrate true masculine feminine balance. However, when humans around them are off centre or there is environmental change bringing in lower vibrations, they are so sensitive that they flip very easily out of balance.

It would help us to tune into the kangaroos and sense how they feel and how they tune into the wind, the earth and the trees.

NEPTUNE

The planet Neptune represents higher spirituality. It is known as the watery planet and named after the God of the Sea, the Elemental Master of Water, Neptune. Water is the medium through which cosmic love is transferred. Much of the water has been frozen on Neptune, holding the wisdom of the ancient civilizations but this has now been energetically released. The colour of this planet is the beautiful blue of higher healing and truth.

~ Rats and Mice ~

These animals originally incarnated with the very spiritual purpose of clearing leftovers. At the same time they were transmuting and purifying lower energies. A well cared-for mouse or rat is an intelligent, much loved pet.

Rats carry disease because they have swept up and taken in human negativity, which has naturally manifested as sickness in their systems. Under normal circumstances they would transmute this but we leave out huge amounts of rubbish and sewage. Also we dislike these rodents. This means they live in fear and cannot transform the lower energies into love, which would enable them to fulfil their divine mission. It would help them and all creatures if we sent them love and appreciation for their work.

VENUS

Venus is the planet of love. It is the fully ascended cosmic heart of this universe and radiates beautiful pink light. Beings who originate from here carry love in their souls.

~ *Guinea pigs* ~

The guinea pigs chose to incarnate in South America because of the quality of love and gentle energy in the land there. Their purpose was to give and receive love. They keep the connection to Venus open, so when you cuddle a guinea pig you receive an input of love from that planet. Contact with a guinea pig is enormously helpful to heal the hearts of abused children.

Guinea pigs link people through Venus to all the stars, planets and galaxies in this universe and are helping to bring the entire universe together with love. One of the reasons they chose to be timid little creatures is so that people will feel empathy towards them.

Wombats from Australia and capibara and agouti from South America are big cousins of the guinea pigs but they do not hold the same qualities.

THE UNIVERSE OF SHEKINAH

Shekinah is a tenth-dimensional universe of love and wisdom. The radiant joy experienced by every being in Shekinah while they are 'at home' is beyond our comprehension. Many of these fast-frequency beings are squeezed in a human body right now, having gone through the veil of illusion, to help Earth in its journey to the fifth dimension. Each of the twelve universes operates in a different dimension. Currently Earth is moving from the third to the fifth dimension. When that happens all the universes will move simultaneously into a faster frequency, so Shekinah will become eleventh-dimensional. The universe then vibrating at the fastest frequency will merge once more with Source and a new one will be born.

~ *Monkeys* ~

All monkeys, including bush babies and lemurs, originate from the tenth-dimensional universe, Shekinah, and they step their frequencies down through the Pleiades. They show us another use of kundalini. By swinging from branch to branch in the trees they demonstrate that it is not necessary to tread on the land to be part of this planet. They are very in tune with the wisdom of the trees.

Monkeys are highly evolved and like the dolphins they would not allow themselves to be caught unless there was a higher purpose for the sacrifice, such as opening the hearts of humanity with compassion.

When they chatter they are bringing forward information from the angels and elements and spreading it to the trees, other animals – and humans, if they listen. The sound made by the howler monkey cleanses your aura.

When they are in the trees they are relaxed and in balance. However, they are very vulnerable when they are not in their true element and are experiencing a different one, for example water or fire. Even on the ground they are vulnerable. But they are on this planet to experience all of these elements because they are not available in their home universe.

They incarnate to experience fun, family life and structure. They are here to learn about life on Earth, not with the intellect of a human, but with the right-brain qualities of unconditional love, acceptance, loyalty and trust.

■ **The KEY of the animals is to honour, respect and embrace the animal kingdom.**

■ **The SOUND is the chatter of monkeys.**

■ **The COLOUR is gold, yellow through to white (the colours of the Universal Angel Fhelyai).**

EXERCISE: *Visualization to understand the spirit of the animals*

1. Find a place where you can be quiet and undisturbed.
2. Light a candle if possible.
3. Relax and close your eyes.
4. Ground yourself by imagining roots going from you deep into the earth.
5. Place Archangel Michael's protective blue cloak around you.
6. Picture yourself in a beautiful place out in nature.
7. Ask the Universal Angel Fhelyai, the angel of animals, to come to you and sense his yellow-to-white light surrounding you.

8. Think of the animal you wish to understand and ask to go to their planet, star or universe of origin.
9. Find yourself in a place that may feel unfamiliar but you are quite safe, held by the Universal Angel Fhelyai.
10. In front of you is the spirit or Higher Self of the animal you asked to know.
11. Take time to communicate with them but most of all listen to what they have to impart to you.
12. Thank them for taking the time and energy to come to you.
13. Sense Universal Angel Fhelyai blessing you and leaving you with love.
14. With new understanding in your heart return to where you started, and open your eyes.

EXERCISE: *To tune into the animals*

1. If you can, go somewhere where you will see animals.
2. Choose one and connect with it from your heart to their heart.
3. Sense how big their Higher Self is and feel their true energy.
4. Tune into the wisdom and knowledge they hold.
5. Honour their courage in coming to Earth.
6. Send them love, respect and thanks.
7. Know that you have made an important connection, which has helped both of you.

EXERCISE: *To listen to the animals*

- Find an animal and listen to the sound it makes. Hear it without question or judgment; just be aware that it is communicating a message. And thank it for this.

The Kingdom of the Ocean Beings

Fish are third- to fifth-dimensional beings while dolphins, whales and turtles are fifth-dimensional. Most of the fish come from the constellation Pisces. Tiny fish are part of a group soul and there could be a thousand of these in one over-soul. Bigger fish like trout could be a group soul of hundred. They are on their way to ascension, as are the big individualized fish such as the dolphins, sharks, whales and rays. The task of the fish is to keep the oceans clean. They also serve the dolphins by bringing in the sonics of the angels and so help to keep the water at a high vibration.

Dolphins are from Lakumay, the ascended aspect of Sirius.

Whales originate from an asteroid in the universe of Shekinah.

Turtles come from Jumbay, the ascended aspect of Jupiter.

Sharks incarnate from Nigellay, the higher aspect of Mars.

They are highly evolved creatures and humans cannot do anything to them without their permission. Whales and dolphins let themselves be beached or come up a river to bring a message to humanity about how we are treating the oceans. Turtles eat polythene bags to show us about the dangers of polluting the oceans and of using plastics.

~ Archangel Joules and the Bermuda Triangle ~

The entire ocean kingdom is in the care of the Universal Angel Joules, whose retreat is the Bermuda Triangle, the important cosmic portal, where the Great Crystal of Atlantis fell. The Bermuda Triangle links Source and the Hollow Earth, bringing seventh-dimensional energy down from Source and up from Hollow Earth. This is particularly important now that the frequency of the planet is rising because the divine blueprint for the oceans is being accessed through this portal. Through joyous laughter and light it radiates higher possibilities through the seas to accelerate the ascension of all water creatures. It also touches humans who venture into or onto the waters.

~ Messages ~

Water cleanses and purifies the planet and is also a conductor of energy. It brings in the messages from other planets, stars, galaxies and the angels. The dolphins, whales, sharks and turtles accept the messages and spread them to all the beings of the ocean kingdom. The communications may be offering enthusiasm, encouragement, inspiration or information. If, for example, a tsunami is about to occur they would advise the fish to move away unless it was their time to pass.

~ Coral reefs ~

In the spiritual realms the angels call coral 'living rock' for it holds the wisdom and knowledge of the ancients that is coming up from Hollow Earth. It also draws nutrients from the earth and the bed of the oceans and transforms them into the life-giving properties of the world's waters.

Where there is living coral there are very fast frequencies. Those fish that live on the coral reefs are all fifth-dimensional.

The coral has a two-way communication flow with Hollow Earth. It not only receives but it also gives information about the oceans. Part of the role of the coral reefs is to keep the waters two parts hydrogen to one part oxygen.

~ Neptune ~

Neptune is the link from the waters of this planet to the universe. Until recently this connection was blocked because the ice on it held the fear of the fall of Atlantis. Thanks to the dedicated spiritual work of many lightworkers and especially the teachers of the Diana Cooper School the ice has melted on that planet. So now information from Atlantis, Lemuria and Mu is once more available and in addition we can access all the wisdom of the universes.

This knowledge has always been held by the dolphins in the water and by the coral of the oceans but it is only now that Neptune has been unlocked that we humans can access it directly from the dolphins. We must also acknowledge the important role the whales, sharks and turtles have played in protecting the angel dolphins and the great wisdom they have held in trust for us for thousands of years.

~ Absorbing the wisdom of Atlantis, Lemuria, Mu and that of the universes ~

Water everywhere is energetically connected. When you drink a glass of pure, cold water, it is linked to the energy of the oceans, so if you are attuned to the fifth dimension and you bless it, you can absorb from it the vast wisdom now available. Tea, hot water or cold water with lemon will not do.

You can also access this wisdom, when you bath, shower or swim in the sea, a clear river or a lake and you bless the water, while your vibration is raised to the fifth dimension. If you are bathing children bless the water, so that they can connect with divine wisdom. And if you are watching children or adults in a swimming pool your blessing will help them all.

If you are not fifth-dimensional the water tries to raise your frequency by transmuting and purifying lower frequencies, even if you do not bless it. Water is composed of two parts hydrogen and one part oxygen; this is metaphorical as well as scientific for the angels say H_2O brings you two parts of hope and one of opportunity.

~ Naming ceremonies with water ~

If you perform your own naming ceremony with pure intent and use blessed water, this will profoundly help the child. Religious ceremonies help too but then the water carries the limitation of the dogma associated with it.

This applies to all ceremonies where blessed water is utilized.

~ Shellfish and elementals ~

The shellfish, prawns, lobsters, shrimps, crabs, cockles, whelks, mussels or oysters are the cleaners of the waters. They perform the same service as the mice and rats in the animal kingdom or the esaks and kyhils in the elemental realms.

Mermaids help the flora and fauna.

~ The Moon ~

All fish are linked to the moon. So are the solid, dependable, gentle turtles. Turtles bring in all the divine feminine qualities even though they lay eggs and do not carry live young. They bring energy through from the moon and use it to teach people, animals and fish. They are helping to bring the planet into the perfect masculine and feminine balance by 2032 for the start of the New Golden Age.

Even the tiny turtles are doing their part. And on land tortoises also bring energies from the moon and spread them.

All the fish as well as the dolphins, whales and turtles hold an aspect of the higher spirituality of the world and by 2032 they will bring it all together, so that the whole can be accessed again.

■ **The KEY of the ocean beings is to drink, bathe in and bless pure water and open yourself to the wisdom of the water kingdom.**

■ **The SOUND is that of whales and dolphins calling.**

■ **The COLOUR is aquamarine.**

EXERCISE: *Visualization to immerse yourself in the energy of water*

1. Find a place where you can be quiet and undisturbed.
2. Light a candle if possible.
3. Relax and close your eyes.
4. Ground yourself by imagining roots growing from your feet deep down into the earth.
5. Place Archangel Michael's blue cloak around you for protection.
6. Picture yourself on a magnificent beach by a clear aquamarine ocean.
7. Invoke the Universal Angel Joules to surround and protect you and feel his energy settle round you.
8. Then move into the water. Whether you can physically swim or not you are totally safe in the ocean with Joules.
9. Let him take you to a coral reef. Float with Joules and enjoy the wonders you see.
10. All the time you are receiving energy and wisdom from the coral.

11. A sea creature approaches you with peace and love.
12. Exchange peace and love with it and listen to its communication.
13. When you are ready thank the sea creature.
14. Joules brings you back to the beach where you sit in the warm sun and reflect on your experience.
15. Thank Joules, bring your awareness back to the present and open your eyes.

EXERCISE: *To create a ceremony with water*

- Remember the phases of the moon are important. New moon is good if you are blessing a new beginning. The full moon confers the wisdom of the divine feminine and much energy.
- Gather a few like-minded people together with the intention of performing a ceremony with water to raise the consciousness.
- Decide on the purpose of the ceremony. It may be to bless a baby, a house, a project, a job or new office. Or you may use it in a Handfast or to bless the trees, a river or a garden.
- Approach the ceremony meaningfully by preparing an altar or a sacred fire. Flowers, candles, joss sticks, appropriate music or articles of beauty or great sentiment help to raise the energy.
- If possible shower and wash your hair. At least wash your hands beforehand. And if possible wear special clothes. If you have nothing particular to don, make sure your clothes are clean and fresh.
- State your intention.
- All bless the water you are using. You may do this with prayers, chanting, toning and singing hymns or bahjans or any other way that feels right for you.
- Sprinkle the water on the person or place you wish to bless. You can also immerse a person totally, if that is right for you.
- Call in the blessings you wish to confer.
- Give thanks.

EXERCISE: *To drink water mindfully*

1. Fill a glass with cold, pure water.
2. Bless it.
3. Imagine this water connecting to the oceans, lakes, rivers, streams, waterfalls and, as you drink it, know that you are one with the wisdom of the cosmic flow of the universe.

The Elemental Kingdom

Elementals are essential for the natural functioning of the planet and it is important to acknowledge that they are there. Some are made up of one element only and others are a combination of several but none have all the elements – earth, air, fire and water – as humans do. There are also wood elementals. Here are the elementals of the different elements:

- Fairies and sylphs are air elementals.
- Goblins, elves, pixies and brownies are earth elementals.
- Mermaids, undines and kyhils are water elementals.
- Salamanders are fire elementals.
- Warburtons are fifth-dimensional wood elementals.
- Fauns, imps and dragons are elementals combining several elements.

Many years ago I saw a fairy in its luminous glory in Findhorn, Scotland, where the veils between the worlds are thin. After that I had no contact with the elementals for many years even though I am in constant contact with angels and unicorns. Then I created a vegetable patch in my garden. As I spent hours digging the soil and watched and tended the seeds and plants I gradually became aware of the little ones. With divine synchronicity people started to send us Orb photographs including many of elementals, which was completely magical. This drew our attention to the myriad of ethereal beings that are helping the planet.

~ Goblins ~

My first contact was with Gobolino, a fifth-dimensional goblin, with a highly developed heart centre, who shared his love and wisdom with me in the woods. I write of this encounter in 2012 and Beyond. He and I have been friends ever since and he sometimes appears in different parts of the world when I am there.

On one occasion I was on holiday in the Arctic with my friend Rosemary Stephenson. We went out at night into the freezing temperatures to walk in the woods and see if we could connect with the elementals. Suddenly I saw Gobolino flickering in and out like a television set with a faulty aerial. Finally he appeared. He had difficulty teleporting into the icy cold. Interestingly, Rosemary did not see him. Her experience was of elves winding up the energy of the portal there.

Apparently souls come here to ascend through the Stellar Gateway of the planet; our Orb photographs confirmed that it was a huge portal where many souls were waiting to pass. One of the services performed by the elves is to keep the energy moving there.

~ Fairies ~

Fairies are beings between the fourth and fifth dimension with many tasks to fulfil. One of them is to look after the growth of flowers and they often also anchor the work of the unicorns and universal angels.

I first met Marigold, one of my fairy acquaintances, in my local forest. As her name suggests she is bright orange. Marigold often slips her little hand into mine as I walk through the woods. At the most unexpected moments I am aware of her presence and we have been known to skip along together. She told me she looks after the marigolds in my vegetable patch.

Marigold first connected with me at the end of autumn, the day after I had pulled up the last of those flowers and thrown them on the compost heap. She explained to me she could have gone to Hollow Earth, in the centre of the Earth for spiritual recuperation but instead she decided to connect with me. I am not sure if this was a good decision for her!

She is light and fun and happy, always laughing but she can be persistent. One day I was walking in the woods with a friend, who had just started on a story when I felt Marigold's hand in mine. I was most surprised as I am rarely aware of the presence of elementals when I am with someone else. She tugged on my hand and I ignored her as politeness dictated I listen to my friend. She pulled again, this time with a sense of urgency. So to my friend I said, 'Excuse me. Sorry to interrupt you. A fairy has a message for me!'

Marigold told me she wished us to stand still as the angels and elementals wanted to anchor a new energy into the woods here. We stood for a few moments until Marigold indicated we could move on.

I asked if it was important that my friend was on the walk with me. Marigold said, 'Yes, because she needs the energy that is coming through.' It turned out that the violet flame was being anchored here so that the negative energy of any person or animal in the woods would be transmuted. The angels and elementals wanted it to be set in the shape of the six-pointed star.

Marigold asked me to place it in the woods and then to walk the star shape consciously invoking the gold and silver violet energy. I was out in the freezing rain the following day calling it in. Interestingly as I reached the far end of the forest, I had the shock of my life. I felt a very large man in a huge cloak bumping into me, intending to knock me over. I jumped and then found my heart thumping. There was no one there! I realized just how important the work must be if beings were trying to frighten me. So I quickly invoked the protection of the Gold Ray of Christ and knew it was safe to continue.

~ Metatron, a fairy and the sound
of elementals singing ~

I particularly want to add this story about a fairy as it illustrates so well the diverse work of the elementals. Before I tell it I must explain that the Universal Angel Metatron always communicates with me through my right ear. No other being ever does so. Kumeka, my guardian angel and other beings telepathically link with me through my left ear and this has always been the case.

It was a wet cold November day but nevertheless it was beautiful in the woods. At the far end where it is quiet a very tall fairy walked up to me. She was about 2ft 6in (75 cm) high and I wondered why she was this big. 'The flower fairies are smaller,' she informed me. 'I am a tree fairy.' I was surprised, as I did not know there were tree fairies. She picked up my thought immediately and explained. 'I work with the lilacs. Really they are bushes.' Indeed she was a lilac colour.

Suddenly I realized she was talking into my right ear and only Metatron ever does this. 'Are you connected to Metatron?' I asked. She laughed. 'I wondered if you would realize. I work with him because he is bringing the frequency of the flowers up to help with the ascension of the planet.'

'I thought fairies worked under the elemental masters and the Universal Angel Purlimiek?'

She was patient. 'Yes, but it is a very human concept to have such a rigid structure. In our dimension we all work for the highest good, so I work with Metatron and Purlimiek in whatever is the best way for the world.'

'I see,' I nodded. It made sense. 'But you are lilac-coloured and Metatron vibrates with orange and gold!'

In the twinkling of an eye the fairy ran along the path in front of me and became a vibrant, bright orange. It startled me. Then she turned to gold. She laughed again and said that Metatron could use any colours to express his purpose and intention and used the sunlight to enable this to happen.

Now Metatron himself stood in a column of orange light by me. He telepathically imparted thanks to me for a piece of work I had done in America and gave me lots of encouragement, so I felt very pleased. He only remained for a moment.

Suddenly my heart opened – the most extraordinary feeling, like a physical opening up from my heart centre to include everything. My heart embraced the birds, the trees, all the people of the world. We were one. I walked slowly along feeling part of the oneness until the feeling faded.

Then I asked the fairy her name. She replied that I could call her Lilac as that was simpler than her real name. Then she jumped up onto my left shoulder and chatted to me in my left ear. She let me know that she had done her job of drawing my attention to Metatron's presence and her connection with

*him by using my right ear and now she could communicate on
my left side! She was clearly happy as she sat on my shoulder
swinging her legs and feeling very relaxed.*

*Then she started to sing. It was so enthralling that I stood
stock-still. I cannot say I heard the sound with my physical
ears. It was in my head somewhere and in my body. Then
hundreds of fairies and other elementals joined in and sang
with her. The sound reverberated through me and it was like
the low hum of millions of distant bees but at a higher pitch. It
came to me that this was the sound of the Key to the elemental
kingdom. It was one of the most amazing experiences of my
life.*

~ The angels work with the elementals ~

This is the story of how working with the energy of an Orb brought the
elementals to me and allowed incredible healing and moving forward
to take place.

*For about two weeks I had been making it my spiritual
practice to breathe in the pink of love and breathe it out to the
trees, rocks, water, flowers, animals, people and everything
around me. One evening I stepped into the darkness of the
garden and took some photographs wondering if any angels
would impress themselves as Orbs into my camera. Three
photos were totally dark and then I saw vivid pink in my next
flash, then black again. I rushed indoors very excited to see
what I had taken and it was the most wonderful Orb I could
imagine. It was Mother Mary in her magenta aspect, the
deepest pink of Archangel Chamuel I have ever seen and an
angel of love! Kumeka told me it was a reward for the love I
had sent out. I was overjoyed. It was so beautiful it softened
my heart and it is a message of love and comfort from the
universe for everyone. I kept breathing it in.*

*A couple of days later I decided to get out into the woods as
early as possible. I visualized the Orb around me as I walked
amongst the trees and sent the pink light out around me.
Suddenly at the far side of the plantation, where few people
walk, I saw an elf wearing a red hat running towards me. He
was surrounded by small children and I realized that they*

were spirit children, who were lost souls who had not passed properly. There were six of them, all looking under the age of five. They seemed quite happy and did not realize that they were dead. Each was accompanied by a thin, transparent green elemental that I assumed were wuryls; they look after stuck souls.

The elf was laughing and jolly. His red hat was like a Father Christmas one, and hung down with a bell on the end of it. The children laughed with joy when he shook it at them.

When they saw me the children ran to me, all except one, who darted into the woodland. But they were looking at the light of Mary and Archangel Chamuel round me. I stood still. My etheric body knelt down and lifted them one by one into the column of light created by Mary and Archangel Chamuel. One little boy was about two, with fair curly hair and wearing an old-fashioned sailor suit. He stretched his arms out, radiant with delight, as an angel brought his mother to take him into the light. As I walked on I thought of the child who had run into the woods and within moments the elf reappeared holding him very firmly by the arm. At the same time he was reassuring him so that the boy was not frightened. He saw Mother Mary's beautiful light and ran to me, so that I could hold him up. He too was collected by his mother and his father.

I looked up into the sky and all six of them came towards me in Orbs to say thank you; I could see their little arms waving. Then a plane flew over leaving a wide, incredibly white trail. As I watched I was told that an angel of love was in the vapour trail escorting the children home. I found myself smiling.

Now I asked the elf why he wore a red hat when I thought elves wore green ones. He replied simply, 'because the children love it.' He told me he had earned the right to help the lost children who did not pass over and his badge of office was the red hat. He also said his name was Bagheer.

You can see the wonderful heart-shaped Orb of Mother Mary, Archangel Chamuel and an angel of love on page 110.

~ Pixies ~

Pixies rove in bands to help maintain the quality of soil. I have not yet seen one but Emily Crosswell, Kathy's daughter, who works in a restaurant near the sea in a lovely town right next to an old ruin and ancient woodlands, told me this story.

> *One evening, soon after she started work at the restaurant, Emily was in the bar when she saw a pixie sitting on some books on her workbench, swinging his feet. He was about 2 ft 6 in (75 cm) tall and had white, peachy skin and big eyes, a bold green. He was wearing dark green tights, a deep red waistcoat, brown-red shorts and a rich green pointed hat. He looked cheery and playful.*
>
> *He came to remind her of the importance of the ancient woodlands, how they need to be nurtured and blessed and asked her to open her heart to them. He said it was important that she allow her true light to shine out and that this could happen more easily if she connected with the ancient land.*
>
> *He also wanted her to be aware that coffee is bad for people and asked her to bless it when she was serving it.*

The elementals work with their tasks in nature but also on many other levels, and they are happy and willing to help humans who are ready. As I am writing this many different kinds of elementals are teleporting from all over the world to help clear the ash of the volcano in Iceland.

■ **The KEY of the elementals is to acknowledge the importance of the elemental kingdom.**

■ **The SOUND is a high-pitched melodious humming.**

■ **The COLOUR is green.**

EXERCISE: *Visualization to open up to the elementals*

1. Find a place where you can be quiet and undisturbed.
2. Light a candle if possible.
3. Relax and close your eyes.

4. Ground yourself by imagining roots going from you deep into the earth.
5. Place Archangel Michael's blue cloak around you for protection.
6. Picture yourself somewhere out in nature, in the forest, by a stream, in the hills, by the sea or even in a park or garden.
7. Open your heart and let one or more elementals come to you. Who are they?
8. Sense their energy and thank them for coming to you.
9. Listen to what they have to say to you.
10. They may want to show you something or take you somewhere. Be open to the experience if this happens.
11. When you are ready, imagine yourself back in the place where you started. Thank the elemental or elementals.
12. Then connect again with your present reality and open your eyes.

EXERCISE: *To connect with elementals*

- Go out into nature and find somewhere where you can blend into the energy of the place you have chosen.
- When you are totally relaxed, feeling at peace and one with all around you, quietly sense if there is an elemental near you.
- You may sense one watching you from a tree or behind a bush or rock.
- Just remain quiet, welcoming and open to anything you may see, sense or feel.

The Angelic Kingdom

The Seraphim are the fastest frequency of the angels. There are 144 of these awesome golden-white beings that surround the Godhead and hold the frequency of Creation at the twelfth-dimensional level. Throughout the universes they sing the thoughts of Source into creation, including the birth of new planets.

They sing the sound *OM* at a frequency we cannot hear. When we chant *OM* while holding an intention we wish to manifest for the highest good, the Seraphim take it and make it work. In many chants *OM* is the active component. As an example, when Australia was being prepared, God had the thought of kangaroos, so the Seraphim sang the energy for them to come to Earth from Nigellay, the ascended aspect of Mars with their specific shape and characteristics.

The crystal chakra that lies between the Stellar Gateway and Source is in the charge of the Seraphim, Seraphina. Here she holds training courses for those who wish to work intergalactically and become Ambassadors for Earth. If your Monad, your divine spark, wishes to do this it attends her training schools. Some of the Monadic energy filters down through your chakras to the part of you that is on Earth. Then you intuitively ask to serve as an intergalactic ambassador during your sleep and your spirit moves into the seventh dimension to do this important work.

~ The numbers of angels in each frequency band

12 is the sacred number of spiritual discipleship. Number 7 influences you to be logical but at the same time to open up to the spiritual knowledge of the higher consciousness.

The angelic realms vibrate to these special numbers. There are 12 x 12 = 144 Seraphim and as the angels slow down their frequency to perform different tasks their numbers multiply by 7. The angels who vibrate at the slowest frequencies nearest to that of humans live in the seventh dimension or seventh heaven.

I was quite bemused by the information that there were specific numbers of angels in each frequency band, all of whom have different tasks. However, we were reminded that everything is evolving at ever-faster frequencies. When a Seraphim's frequency becomes fast enough it is absorbed into the Godhead and another speeds up its vibration to take its place. This continues throughout the angelic realms, right down to the elementals.

~ Cherubim ~

The Cherubim vibrate at the eleventh-dimensional frequency. There are 7 x 144 of them, which is 1008. They hold the energy of pure love between and around the planets, stars and galaxies. We describe this special love in Key 46. They also help with the growth of the entire stellar world and help to develop the qualities of the different planets. They take the harmonic frequencies of the Seraphim and bring them to the slower vibratory level where they can become matter. Other angels take the energies further down the frequency band until they can physically manifest on Earth as something humans can touch and feel.

~ Powers ~

The Powers vibrate at the tenth-dimensional frequency. There are 7 x 7 x 144 of them, which is 7056.

The Powers are Lords of Karma as well as angels of birth and death for the entire universe. They work with the timings of birth and death so that the soul can catch the cosmic currents and have time to re-integrate when they return to spirit. They also oversee the healing of the soul.

The moment of birth is most important and is very carefully chosen by the incoming soul, its angels and guides. It launches the child into its destiny. I remember when a baby was overdue and something prompted me to suggest we chant for its safe arrival. The mother, father and I started to chant Om namo bhagavate vasudevaya and we did so for an hour. Then the expectant mother went to bed and her partner and I continued for another hour or so. He said he literally felt the

*baby's soul respond and then it arrived very quickly. Kumeka
told me that incoming soul was indeed going to be late and the
angels impressed on me to chant in order to call it. My guide
said that if we had not chanted the baby would have been
born safely but the planetary alignment it had chosen and
therefore its destiny would have been affected. Om, the sound
of creation, is very powerful.*

The Powers co-ordinate with other universes, for example, if a soul
wishes to incarnate on Earth or experience Saturn, these highly evolved
angelic beings will take the decisions. With some people the Intergalactic Council has the final say.

Kathy's guide, Wywyvsil is a power, who runs teaching schools in
the inner planes to support beings and angels from all over the universes. Some of these courses are to prepare them for experiences in the
different planets, stars and galaxies as well as the angelic realms.

The Powers also direct and guide some of the high-frequency humans who are beings of the universe.

The Powers keep the Akashic Records of all that happens, which
are stored in the Great Pyramid of Hollow Earth. The karmic records
for all individual beings that live in or visit this universe are held in
the Golden Globe within the Seventh Heaven, which is looked after
by Sanat Kumara. The universal computer for all the universes is held
within a mutable Golden Globe within Source.

~ Thrones ~

The Thrones vibrate at the ninth-dimensional frequency. There are 7 x
7 x7 x144 of them at any given time, which is 49,392.

They ensoul the stars and planets. They hold the blueprint from
Source of the star or planet in their charge and their heart becomes the
hollow centre of it. When a universe is ready to move into the fifth dimension the Thrones sing the harmonies for this to happen. Then they
hold the note at a faster vibration for its ascension. They continuously
sing the note of ascension and this is the sound of the cosmic heart,
which is like an orchestra of harps. These beings perform the work of
holding an aspect of creation with the greatest joy and delight.

They can affect the creation they hold. For example, Gaia has open-
heartedly welcomed beings from all over the universes and agreed to
the experiment of free will and so has had to work very hard to balance

the masculine and feminine energy. Because Earth is the spiritual solar plexus of the universe and holds the fear for all the stars and planets, she has had to transmute all that she has received from them. She must also keep a balance with all other planets.

The Harmonic Convergence in 1987 was hugely beneficial for Earth when, as a result of all the prayers and meditations of humanity, Source returned the violet flame of transmutation for the use of everyone. With the help of the violet flame negative energy can be transmuted into positive, darkness into light, karma released.

The other stars, planets and galaxies are also working to stay in balance. They must bring in Source energy and pass it on. The Thrones keep the balance of giving and receiving in the universe.

Humans have twelve spiritual chakras but also many lesser chakras, such as those in the hands, feet, elbows and other places. When the main twelve are in balance and harmony the others are too. It is the same in the universe. When the specific stars, planets and galaxies that are the 12 spiritual chakras stay in harmony it helps all the other stellar connections to do so too for they are all minor chakras.

~ The Principalities ~

The Principalities are seventh- to ninth- dimensional angels. There are 7 x 7 x 7 x 7 x 144 of them at any given time, which is 345,744. They are in charge of huge projects such as big schools and businesses and are overseeing the end story of dinosaur businesses and financial institutions of this age. They are facilitating the concept of the new business paradigm, fifth-dimensional communities and Golden Cities for the forthcoming Golden Age. For this, they co-ordinate elementals, angels, animals and humans to be in the right place at the right time. They also work with the Thrones to ensure the time and place is aligned with the highest good of the planet.

Principalities are in charge of each of the indigenous cultures and also of countries.

~ Unicorns ~

Unicorns are fully of the angelic realms and, like the Principalities, vibrate between the seventh- and ninth- dimensional frequencies though we can only connect with them at the seventh dimension. The spiralling horn, which radiates from their third eyes is really pure energy and indicates their level of enlightenment. With it they open hearts, give healing and pour light into people, places and situations. They are known as the purest of the pure, bringing enlightenment, innocence and purity back to Earth. They were present in the Golden Era of Atlantis but when the frequency declined they had to withdraw. Now we have raised the vibration of the planet so that they can return to help us.

They assist us energetically to fulfil the true desires of our souls. Their energy is vast, gentle yet powerful and they often connect with people while they are asleep to help them reach their potential.

If you have a desire to help others, nature or the animal kingdom, they will be supporting you.

~ Universal angels and archangels ~

Universal angels and archangels are seventh- to eighth- dimensional angels but they have different roles. There are 7 x 7 x 7 x 7 x 7 x 144 of them at any given time, which is 2,420,208.

~ Universal angels ~

The names of many of the universal angels are familiar to us and they fulfil a number of tasks.

~ Universal angels who oversee the different seasons ~

Universal Angel Gabriel looks after spring. He sends the snow to purify the land in preparation for the new season and pure white snowdrops to cleanse us, bring us joy and raise our spirits.

Universal Angel Mariel looks after the energies of summer. It is in the warmth and sunlight that people open up to each other and their souls expand.

Universal Angel Aurora, the twin flame of Uriel, watches over autumn.

Universal Angel Sandalphon takes care of the energies of winter when everything is asleep deep under the earth.

~ Universal angels who look after each of the continents ~

Continent	Universal Angel overseeing
Africa	Uriel and also Afra
America and Canada	Michael
Central and South America and the Caribbean	Chamuel
Australia	Roquiel
Europe	Raphael
Asia	Jophiel
Arctic and Antarctic	Gabriel
The whole world	Metatron and Sandalphon
The oceans	Joules

~ Universal angels who look after other aspects of the world ~

Aspect	Universal Angel
Animals	Fhelyai
Music	Sandalphon
Trees and nature	Purlimiek
Stars and the cosmos	Butyalil
Hollow Earth	Gersisa
The entity of Earth	Lady Gaia
Bringing compassion and love across the universes	Mother Mary
Linking all the stars and planets	Metatron

~ Archangels ~

The archangels direct the angels and hold the higher qualities for them. For example, if humanity sends enough prayers for peace into a particular region, the archangels will send the angels of peace there and hold the divine vision of harmony.

I have often noticed the archangels entering a seminar hall before it begins. They remain holding the vision for the day, while hundreds and sometimes thousands of their angels work with individuals who attend.

~ Angels ~

The angels vibrate at the seventh dimension, normally beyond our range of vision and hearing. There are 7 x 7 x 7 x 7 x 7 x 7 x 144 = 16,941,456 of them and they have many tasks, including looking after humans. There are angels of love, angels of mercy, angels of peace amongst others, all doing their work and all helping to smooth our lives. And, of course, there are the guardian angels.

~ Guardian angels ~

The guardian angels vibrate at the slowest frequency of the seventh dimension and are appointed as guardians because they can most closely match our level and so connect more easily with us. Your guardian angel is with you throughout your incarnations on Earth and loves you with deep commitment. They are androgynous like all beings of the angelic realms and totally in balance with their masculine and feminine energies. They help you fulfil your divine blueprint for your life by arranging co-incidences, meetings and setting up situations to help you develop or go down the right path for you. If you use your free choice unwisely they whisper higher possibilities to you. If it is not your time to die, your guardian angel will save you. Your angel will help you in any way as long as it is for your highest good but you must ask.

My friend Rosemary had landed in a small airport and then had to take two buses to her destination. She chatted to the driver of the first one who helped her with her case when it was time to change in the middle of nowhere. As she watched the bus drive away over the hill she realized she had left her handbag on it, containing all her money, her passport, her mobile phone, her ongoing tickets, everything. She felt panic rising, her knees going weak and her heart thumping. What on earth was she going to do? She forced herself to breathe deeply. Then she called in Archangel Michael to help her.

A few minutes later she saw a bus coming over the hill. The driver has felt a sudden impulse to look back and had seen her handbag on the seat. He felt impelled to bring it back to her! Clearly Archangel Michael had impressed on him to take this action.

~ Orbs ~

Orbs are the sixth-dimensional light bodies of beings of the angelic realms. They have brought their frequency down to a level where it can be caught on film. I find it fascinating that they are so dedicated to helping us, and the planet's progress, that they are willing to do this so that we can see them and access their energy in photographs. Looking at Orbs is another way to connect with angelic energy for their message and their light continues to radiate out from the picture. Below you can see an Orb with the vibration of the Archangels Zadkiel and Gabriel.

■ **The KEY of the Angelic Kingdom is to ask for the highest good.**

■ **The SOUND is that of an orchestra of harps.**

■ **The COLOUR is gold.**

Archangel Zadkiel with an angel of Gabriel and a unicorn. As you look at it you receive deep purification and cleansing.

Photograph by Lynn Ogilvie

EXERCISE: *Visualization to connect with your guardian angel*

1. Find a place where you can be quiet and undisturbed.
2. If possible, light a candle.
3. Relax and close your eyes.
4. Ground yourself by imagining roots going from your feet deep into the earth.
5. Place Archangel Michael's blue cloak of protection around you.
6. Breathe the colour gold into your aura until you sense you are in a golden egg.
7. Ask your guardian angel or any other angel to touch you.
8. You may sense yourself enfolded in love or peace, feel a touch, smell a perfume or have no conscious reaction. Just know the angel is with you and relax into the energy.
9. The angel may give you a message so remain open to this.
10. When you are ready to return to waking consciousness, thank the angel and open your eyes.

EXERCISE: *To connect with the angels through Orbs*

Look at the picture of an Orb, for instance the one on the previous page. You can find ascension Orbs and others in our books *Ascension Through Orbs* and *Enlightenment Through Orbs*. There are also a huge variety of them on the *Orbs Cards* or on our websites *www.dianacooper.com* or *www.kathycrosswell.com*. Here are some ways of working with them.

– Breathe in the energy of the Orb.
– Place the Orb picture to your heart and notice the sensation you have.
– Hold the picture of the Orb in your third eye as you meditate on it.
– Imagine you are within the Orb and walk in it or spend time sensing its light round you.
– When you place the photograph of someone or their name on an Orb picture, they will receive the energy of the angelic being.
– For protection place the picture or name on an Orb of Archangel Michael.
– For enlightenment or those whose souls have withdrawn slightly such as many autistic children place the picture or name on a unicorn Orb.

- For healing place the picture or name on an Orb of Archangel Raphael.
- For new children who are ungrounded and cannot access the wisdom of their higher selves place the picture or name on an Orb of the Universal Angels Jophiel and Sandalphon.
- For ascension place the picture or name on an Orb of the Universal Angel Metatron.

The Deva Kingdom

Devas are seventh-, eighth- and ninth- dimensional beings who work with the blueprint of creation.

~ Ninth-dimensional devas ~

These are the visionaries who work with Pan and the Universal Angel Butyalil on the cosmic blueprint. They make sure every star and planet is in its rightful place. They hold and manage the wisdom of the entire cosmos, checking that everything works with perfect harmony and synchronicity. For example, a shooting star fulfils many functions; burns out a star that is no longer needed, creates a space that other stars can expand into, sends a message across the heavens of endings and new beginnings and reminds us that everything is in perfect divine order. Devas can change blueprints if it is necessary.

Devas are working with Earth to bring the planet to ascension so that the whole universe can move into a higher frequency. This in turn impacts on other universes and is raising the vibration of the entire cosmos. This development is starting to take place in 2012 at the end of a 260,000-year cosmic era.

~ The in-breath of God ~

During the in-breath everything comes closer to God. This eleven-year period from 2012 to 2023 is the shake-up during which all is enhanced. It is time to step up to the mark, so it is important to live the qualities we discuss for Golden Earth. When you do so everything becomes lighter and clearer. You feel more alive and vibrant. If you do everything in accordance with the higher precepts you will live in harmony and joy. And you are asked to embrace and bless those who need to be held in the highest light.

~ Eighth-dimensional devas ~

These are a group of high-frequency beings who enthusiastically teach about the visions. They pour love into new concepts as they come into creation. For example, where a new star is coming into form they hold the vision of it being filled with divine love. If a new kind of animal is to incarnate on Earth they hold the image of it fitting into the blueprint of our planet with love.

They teach those of the angelic realms who will be looking after the concept about the blueprint and how to fill it with love. If it is a flower they will teach Dom, the Elemental Master of Air, who is a seventh-dimensional being, about it. If it is to be a new way of being, such as the end of apartheid, they will teach a Universal Angel. The unicorns help the people who are handling the blueprint to hold it in the purest light.

~ Seventh-dimensional angelic devas ~

The angelic devas take the vision and put it into practice. After the in-breath of God there is a nine-year period to stabilize and find our strengths. During this period we are particularly asked to work with the seventh dimensional angelic devas to build the new. It will be a time of rejuvenation, to start again with vitality and enthusiasm.

The angelic devas work with God to bring forth new and higher blueprints for the whole of creation, throughout the universes. Source holds the vision for the new blueprint for humanity whilst the devas implement it. For example, if someone has a vision of creating a community, the angelic devas help with the practicality of bringing it to fruition.

At this level of creation the masculine and feminine must be in balance. If, for example, a couple wants a baby at the eighth dimensional level they would be excited and chatting about it. Then at the seventh dimension you need male and female to conceive it and bring it to birth.

In their quest for knowledge humans have changed the divine blueprints of many animals and other aspects of nature. As they lost their connection with Source they forgot the wider vision of the universe and how everything was designed to work in harmony. If we had maintained our connection we would have accessed all the knowledge we desired without tampering with the divine blueprint.

The Reptile Kingdom

~ Snakes, alligators, crocodiles, lizards,
komodo dragons, tortoises, turtles ~

The reptiles still maintain their original divine blueprint. They all come from other universes and step their energy down through Neptune to bring the wisdom of Lemuria and Atlantis through with them.

We were asked to write about them in this chapter on devas because they carry pure Source energy, the original divine energy. They know who they are and what they are here for. They do and be, act and relax, in accordance with their innate instincts, not deviating to fit in with others. They are who they are exactly in tune with their blueprint.

All the various elementals work with the different reptiles.

Snakes come to humans to tell them to look beyond the obvious and see the truth that lies behind it. This may be a warning, a wake-up call or a reminder. They represent metamorphosis and nudge you that it is time to change or that it is safe to move on. They are a potent protection symbol and their energy holds you in safety against human mischief. The ability to be with them without fear is an ancient high initiation for they sense fear and react to it.

Reptiles have no emotions or attachments yet they feel the heartbeat of the Earth. Because they are so close to the ground, they are constantly in touch with the energy of the soil and through it into Hollow Earth.

In the case of turtles, they are totally at one with the ocean and the land, entrusting their eggs to the latter. They are in tune with the moon, the currents and the whole natural world. They radiate this knowing wherever they are.

All reptiles draw in the Atlantean and Lemurian wisdom from Hollow Earth as well as the knowledge of many of the ancient tribes. Then they exude this for others to experience without them realizing it. They also draw wisdom from their planets of origin and from Neptune through their bodies into Hollow Earth. There it is taken into the huge crystal, then transferred to the crystal on top of the central pyramid, which directs it out through the twelve portals to the various stars.

■ **The KEY of the devas and the reptile kingdom is to discover your original divine blueprint.**

■ **The SOUND for the devas is the sounds of the qualities taken up on the breath to a higher level.**

■ **The COLOUR is gold.**

EXERCISE: *Visualization to bring in something new for the benefit of the planet*

1. Find a place where you can be quiet and undisturbed.
2. Light a candle if possible.
3. Relax and close your eyes.
4. Ground yourself by imagining roots going from you deep into the earth.
5. Place Archangel Michael's blue cloak around you for protection.
6. Ask to be shown the vision of something new for the benefit of the planet.
7. Picture it and call on the seventh-dimensional devas to bring it into manifestation.
8. Ask the eighth-dimensional devas to fill it with love.
9. Call in Pan and the Universal Angel Butyalil to hold it in divine cosmic order.
10. Hold over your vision the symbol of the six-pointed star.
11. Thank the universe for this opportunity to serve.
12. Then connect again with your waking reality and open your eyes.

EXERCISE: *To tune into the blueprint of creation*

Decide on an aspect of creation that you would like to explore. Then tune into its divine blueprint with love and respect to feel what it is all about and what qualities its blueprint carries. For example, think about a tree and tune into the following aspects:

- Its height, width, length of life and the depth of its roots.
- Its bark and why it has its particular qualities.
- Its connection to Hollow Earth and how it maintains this.
- The way it transfers its wisdom.
- The energies it passes to humans and animals.
- How it works with the elementals.
- The offering it gives after death.

EXERCISE: *To tune into the reptiles*

Draw a reptile and as you do so focus on its particular energies and message.

Sirius

The star system of Sirius is helping Earth to ascend. Part of it, known as Lakumay, has already ascended and is operating at a very high frequency. The beings of Sirius have developed their higher minds and those incarnating on Earth are bringing forward new advanced concepts. In addition, an understanding of spiritual technology is held here. Many highly evolved souls from all over the universes are learning about this in the training schools and universities of Sirius before they incarnate on Earth to bring it forward for the New Golden Age.

Each of the twelve aspects in this section is a Key to part of the wisdom of Sirius. When you fully understand and access all of them you become a Master of the Universe. When you hear the twelve keys sounded together you start to open your consciousness to higher awareness and advanced concepts.

■ **The KEY of Sirius is to understand the Universal Metatron Cube.**

■ **The SOUND for this Golden Cosmic Key is the cosmic orchestra of all the sounds.**

■ **The COLOUR is blue green.**

Time and Speed

Time is not linear. It speeds up as your consciousness rises and this is one way of telling where your consciousness is at any moment. If you are, for example, standing in the rain waiting for transport that is late and are thinking grumpy thoughts about your boss because you are sure you will not get a pay rise because you do not deserve one, time will crawl by very slowly indeed. You will probably feel every drip of water down the back of your neck. If you are really impatient because you are racing against a deadline to catch a plane and find yourself stuck in a traffic jam, time will dawdle past, as it will if you are impatiently waiting for a letter to arrive. If, on the other hand, you are happily absorbed in what you are doing, time will race by. When you are in love time flies for you are in a high state of consciousness during which you see the divine in another.

As the consciousness of the people on the planet has risen over the last fifty years, time has sped up.

However, some of the inventions that enable us to do more in less time are not necessarily in tune with the rising frequency of the planet. For example e-mails allow us instant communication, while jet planes fly us quickly around the world. As a result our expectations are for instant gratification and this may not be in alignment with the flow of energy of the universe. When people ask the spirit world about timing it is often notoriously inaccurate. This is because when spirit says, 'Soon,' we expect that to mean tomorrow, while to them it means when the energy is right.

Our impatience and expectations put us under pressure. Your stress will not make the transport arrive more quickly, dissolve the traffic jam or deliver the letter to your door a second earlier than divine timing dictates. It resists the process. Only raising your consciousness can put you into the perfect flow. Watch nature and the grace with which it blossoms and fades. Observe how the turtles catch a current in the ocean and flow with it. They relax and let go, so that it takes them to the perfect place in divine timing.

Go with the flowing breath of the planet.

~ Time in the third dimension ~

In the third dimension we consciously hold onto the old flight or fight instincts. When we resist, our low frequency response stops the flow of what is happening. This means that we create choppy waves, which results in a rough ride through time. When we bless people and situations we swim with a calm ocean.

For example, you have a business plan with someone and that person does something dishonest which puts your idea into jeopardy. In the third dimension your anger keeps you back and the plan does not come to fruition. In the fifth dimension you bless your partner with integrity and light, while continuing to maintain your vision. It then comes about.

All unresolved business holds time back while letting it go allows you to enter the flow again. If you hold a grudge it must eventually be resolved but you may like to ask how long you are prepared to hold back your joy; a week? A year? A lifetime? Ten lifetimes? All emotions and material possessions that we grasp affect the physical body and make us ill. When we let go our body realigns with the natural flow of time.

~ Time in the fourth dimension ~

In the fourth dimension time is affected by the fact that you are aware of a situation but you are not doing anything about it. You are seeing but not acting.

~ Time in the fifth dimension ~

In the fifth dimension you are truly flowing with the universe. You are never impatient or in a hurry because you know that you will arrive in perfect divine timing. If a happening apparently holds you back you are happily aware that you have something to learn or that everything is unfolding perfectly. You trust the universe to serve your highest good.

~ *Time in the sixth dimension* ~

1. You have your feet on the earth but your consciousness is elsewhere, in other words you are experiencing two realities at the same time.

   One day I was walking in my local forest when a unicorn appeared in front of me and invited me to ride with it. I immediately accepted and found myself perched on its back. At the same time I was aware of my feet on the ground, the trees, the flowers and everything about me. A lady with a dog walked towards me and the unicorn moved away through the trees. I watched as it carried part of me away. My conscious awareness stayed in my body as I walked. When the lady had passed, the unicorn returned and again part of me walked while another part of me rode on its back. Later I was told that the dog could sense the unicorn and was unsettled by its high energy, so the mighty being moved away.

2. You are in the sixth dimension when you psychically see your own future with your impact on the planet and bless it.

3. You experience the sixth dimension when you walk with the angels and masters and align your energy with theirs.

It is human nature to focus on this latter aspect of the sixth dimension but we are asked to say that the first and second are most important for living the frequency of this dimension.

~ *Time in the seventh dimension* ~

These are enlightenment experiences, moments of oneness. If you feel total peace and completely in tune with your surroundings you are in the seventh dimension.

I was told that the wonder and awe I felt when I first met my guide, Kumeka, made it a seventh-dimensional time. When Kathy and I were asked to write the Orbs books, the world stood still for us, and we were in divine bliss. Kathy sat on the cliffs overlooking the sea one day and let go of everything. In that instant she was in this high frequency.

■ **The KEY is to let go and go with the flow.**

■ **The SOUND is that of silence.**

■ **The COLOUR is crystal clear.**

EXERCISE: *Visualization to flow towards your vision*

1. Find a place where you can be quiet and relaxed.
2. Light a candle if possible. Let yourself relax and close your eyes.
3. Ground yourself by imagining roots going from you deep into the earth, anchoring you there.
4. Place Archangel Michael's blue cloak around you.
5. Picture your vision.
6. Are you tied to any people or stuck emotions that are holding you back? If so, see them like balls and chains and ask Archangel Michael to cut them away.
7. Is there anything else preventing your dream from coming true? Picture yourself releasing it.
8. Now feel your vision as if it is already happening.
9. Notice how you feel. Are you ready to accept this wonder, excitement or satisfaction in your life?
10. If you are not, re-do the visualization as many times as you need to. If you are ready to accept it, enjoy creating your vision.
11. Return to your waking reality and open your eyes.

EXERCISE: *To release what holds you back and causes time to slow down for you*

1. Write down your vision.
2. Write all the feelings, emotions or factors that are holding you back.
3. Take decisions about letting them go.

EXERCISE: *Chanting Om when you are held back*

When you are in a traffic jam or held up by forces outside your control, relax and chant *Om* either aloud or under your breath. Notice what happens to time.

Other Dimensions –
Ascended Masters,
Higher Self, Monad

~ Multi-dimensional beings ~

We are all multi-dimensional beings. While some parts of us are in the third, fourth or fifth dimension, there are aspects of us in much higher dimensions. This applies to most of us.

You may be third-, fourth- or fifth- dimensional on Earth but your Higher Self or soul is always seventh-dimensional or higher. Your Monad or I AM presence, your original divine spark, is always twelfth-dimensional, for it is the Source energy once diluted, just as a child is one step away from the energy of its parent.

~ Babies and children ~

As innocent babies and children we are in a higher dimension. Then for most of us we move into lower ones as we become older and experience life's challenges. When we realize who we are and become more spiritual, our vibration rises again.

~ The sixth dimension ~

In order to have moments of being an ascended master you must be able to bring the sixth-dimensional frequency into your body. People can flip easily between dimensions and the fact that you are in the sixth dimension for a while with your feet in both worlds does not mean you are a master. Many people with Down's syndrome or who have learning difficulties have high frequencies because they see the joy, laughter and beauty in all things but they are not ascended masters. No one has ever maintained ascended mastery while in a body, not even during the

Golden Era of Atlantis. The High Priests and Priestesses were very close to doing so but even they had moments of doubt, which brought their frequencies down. However, when you aspire to maintain this dimension as much as possible you will impact very powerfully and positively on other people.

~ The seventh dimension ~

To be a fully ascended master you must be able to live in the seventh dimension and this can only happen when you have left your body.

In order to come to Earth your soul must be in the seventh dimension or higher. If you come from another universe or are of a very high frequency, you move from your home planet to one of the ascension planets, stars or galaxies, Neptune, Orion, Sirius or the Pleiades before conception. This is to prepare yourself for your forthcoming experience on the 'heavy' planet Earth. Your frequency lowers as you come into incarnation.

~ In the womb ~

While they are in the womb the frequency of souls varies. When they contact the mother before conception they have usually transformed down to the fifth dimension so that their spiritual communication can take place.

Some connect with the mother at conception and move into the fifth dimension as they stay near her during pregnancy, then they move into a lower dimension soon after birth.

Others connect with the mother at differing times during the pregnancy and move into the fifth dimension at that time.

During pregnancy the energy of the mother is really important. She needs to be ready, physically, emotionally, mentally and spiritually.

If the mother feels sick it is because the frequency of the incoming soul is higher than her own at that moment. She needs to raise her vibration by walking in nature to ground herself, drinking blessed water, eating healthily, meditating and undertaking good spiritual practices.

Emotionally it is important to feel grateful and honoured to have the spiritual responsibility of looking after this particular soul. She must live with love, compassion, patience, joy and laughter and be happy with who she is. Both parents need to live their truth in order to offer the best for the child.

Mentally, be positive and send good thoughts and a welcome to the soul of the child. Be inclusive and acknowledge his or her wisdom. For example listen to them telling you of the food they do not like.

Spiritually understand that the child is a being in its own right. You make choices for the foetus so choose food, drink and the environment it is coming into for its highest good. Be happy!

~ After birth ~

When the baby is born it is essential to keep the frequency high and this will mostly be done as it was during pregnancy. But now it will have a huge impact how you attend to the physical needs and the environment, as well as how you live your life.

It is the responsibility of the parents to put psychic protection round the child, to keep it safe from lower thought forms or entities and also to protect its spirit while it travels to its home planet for spiritual sustenance while it is asleep.

~ To help the trauma of birth ~

The physical space needs to be soft, warm and welcoming. In addition, if the mother asks her soul to link to the baby's soul as it is born, an information exchange takes place, which will help the baby.

The mother can also ask her guardian angel and the baby's guardian angel to work together; this can be of enormous benefit.

~ The Monad or I AM Presence ~

This is the original divine spark from God to which you belong. It is twelfth-dimensional. It is unconditional love, pure agape, unquestioning, androgynous and it contains the ultimate manual to maintain divine beauty, wisdom, harmony, grace and light. All you need is there and you can connect to this aspect of yourself when you open the Stellar Gateway, the twelfth and highest chakra.

All Monads are the same. They are Source energy, once diluted. How you choose to access and use this energy makes you who you are.

Just as Source shares out equal amounts of its energy to Monads, they in turn send out twelve aspects to become souls to experience the different dimensions and ultimately to bring their accumulated knowledge and wisdom back to the Monad.

Because our planet is struggling with ascension there are no more Monads being created here. However if Earth easily and triumphantly ascends, then more Monads will be created.

~ The Soul or Higher Self ~

Your soul, an aspect of your Monad or I AM Presence, is sent down to experience life in different dimensions.

~ What will happen to third-dimensional beings in this universe? ~

I always thought that those third-dimensional beings that were unable or unwilling to raise their frequency before the New Golden Age would move to another third-dimensional planet to continue their ascension. However, we have been told that if they originate in this universe they will return to the spiritual planes for training and healing, until they are ready to return to Earth at a higher frequency.

Those third-dimensional beings that do not raise their frequency and are not from this universe will continue their experiences on another third-dimensional planet in a different universe.

The energy of people who cannot maintain the fourth dimension would have a negative effect on Earth.

The Spiritual Dimensions

~ The behaviour and patterning of the third dimension ~

Because this book is fifth-dimensional we have been asked to present this information within an exercise.

1. Relax and ask Archangel Sandalphon to place a fifth-dimensional bubble over you.
2. About the third dimension. Those who live at this level are self-centered. They do not empower others but are greedy, ambitious, fearful or doubtful. Their thoughts are negative and they see the lowest in people and situations.
3. When you have finished reading this, cleanse yourself of any

third-dimensional energy you may have picked up by invoking the gold and silver violet flame and breathing its energy into your cells.

~ *Dark souls* ~

As with the information about third-dimensional souls, ask Archangel Sandalphon to place you in a fifth-dimensional bubble before you read this. After you have read this information please cleanse yourself of any lower energy you may have absorbed.

If a person is dark, at the end of their incarnation they return to their soul, which has to purify the energy. The angels help with this.

If the darkness is too much and would overwhelm the soul something different happens and here is a story to illustrate it.

> *One day Kathy was in her garage with someone who was also psychic. They saw a bad Pharaoh contained within a pyramid. He pushed his energy forward as if trying to get out of the enclosing shape and they saw his face. Then suddenly he was shoved back in. Kathy and her friend were told that he would not be allowed anywhere near Earth because he would do too much damage. Twelve years later after much healing and education in the inner planes, he was released.*

Something similar has happened with Hitler. He is contained in a pyramid and not allowed to return to his soul. If he returned to his soul, even if he did not reincarnate, he could influence people with his energy. His soul was very aware of what happened and decided it needed to learn about love in order to raise its frequency. Therefore another aspect of Hitler's soul has incarnated in South America to a mother who knows how to love, so that he can experience this. Then he can take love back to the soul to expand its light levels.

Because this planet and this universe are ascending these dark souls are going to a special school in the inner planes to receive healing and teaching.

~ The behaviour and patterning
of the fourth dimension ~

At this level the heart is opening and you recognize your soul is on an eternal journey, not just for this life. You are not yet ready to take responsibility for what this means but you start to understand it.

~ The behaviour and patterning
of the fifth dimension ~

You are working for the highest good of everyone and the planet with your heart open.

~ The behaviour and patterning
of the sixth dimension ~

You have feet in both worlds and focus on the love of the planet and all on her.

~ The behaviour and patterning
of the seventh dimension ~

You are walking with the angels and masters. Beings from the Pleiades are seventh-dimensional.

~ The behaviour and patterning
of the eighth dimension ~

You are accepting yourself as a cosmic being. Beings from Venus, such as Jesus, Isis and Aphrodite are ninth-dimensional.

A high-frequency person can maintain the twelfth dimension for moments, for example as they channel a twelfth-dimensional being. The only person we know from the twelfth dimension is Babaji, the great master.

~ Kathy and Diana's personal experiences ~

When I left my soul and incarnated, all aspects of my soul had an equal share of the energy. Three of the aspects remained with my soul to support me. One came to Earth with me, the

175

others are in another universe. As my life and work developed I agreed to take responsibility for the lives of all the other aspects and for their ascension. In exchange they gave me their energy. Because I have now raised my frequency I am told I can now give back their energy and still fulfil my pathway, so I have started this process. Ultimately this will help all the aspects and my soul.

Kathy has seven aspects of her soul actively supporting her life path. A few remain in her soul while the remainder are not in this universe.

Our respective Monads are feeding energy to both of us.

■ **The KEY is to live your truth.**

■ **The SOUND is that of one tap on a crystal bowl.**

■ **The COLOUR is transparent white.**

EXERCISE: *Visualization to experience the seventh dimension*

1. Find a place where you can be quiet and undisturbed.
2. Raise the vibration by lighting a candle if possible.
3. Relax and close your eyes.
4. Ground yourself by imagining roots going from your feet deep into the earth.
5. Place Archangel Michael's blue cloak around you.
6. Surround yourself in gold light and sense the angels surrounding you.
7. Call in the Universal Angel Gabriel and feel his wondrous wings around you, soft and warm.
8. Ask him to take you to the seventh dimension, the seventh heaven and feel yourself rising up in his arms.
9. When you reach the seventh heaven totally surrender yourself into the love and joy of the angels and unicorns.
10. There is nothing to do; nowhere to go. Simply let go and be.
11. When it is time to return, Archangel Gabriel is bringing you back to where you started.
12. Once you open your eyes, take time to adjust into your life.

Other Planets, Stars and Galaxies

The fifth-dimensional planetary chakras round the world are programmed to awaken and light up in 2012.

However, planets, stars and galaxies are all cosmic chakras. Some of them are multi-dimensional and they connect to and bring light into those on the planet. Those that we discuss in this chapter all have an ascended part that is seventh-dimensional. These higher aspects have always been open and are holding steady the light and wisdom for this universe. They are maintaining the highest vision and the divine blueprint for the cosmos.

~ The Cosmic Earth Star Chakra ~

Neptune is the transformer through which the wisdom of Atlantis and Lemuria is downloaded to us at a level we can accept. Its ascended aspect Toutillay holds the cosmic light for this universe.

~ The Cosmic Base Chakra ~

Quishy is the ascended aspect of Saturn. It is radiating the energy of spiritual discipline to enable us to fulfil our divine potential and to enjoy all the wonders of being on Earth by linking us to our original divine essence.

~ The Cosmic Sacral Chakra ~

Lakumay is the ascended aspect of Sirius. It has already started to bring in the energy of transcendent love. By 2032 this higher love will have spread to most parts of the planet and then people will express pure love through sexuality.

~ The Cosmic Navel Chakra ~

The Sun is the navel chakra of this universe and it beams to us the ability to go out and actively make people feel welcome. The energy coming in will open people up to beings from other planets and enable us on Earth to accept their wisdom.

~ The Cosmic Solar Plexus Chakra ~

Pilchay is the ascended aspect of Earth and this holds the cosmic wisdom waiting to come in.

~ The Cosmic Heart Chakra ~

The cosmic heart chakra is Venus and this brings love directly from God.

~ The Cosmic Throat Chakra ~

Telephony is the ascended aspect of Mercury and this chakra encourages telepathic communication with the masters and angels on the Golden Ray. It also enables advanced communication with humans, animals, trees and all life forms. It brings back the qualities of the Golden Era of Atlantis, such as levitation, teleportation, telekinesis and the telepathic sending of healing.

~ The Cosmic Third Eye Chakra ~

Jumbay is the ascended aspect of Jupiter and this brings in huge amounts of wisdom, joy and expansion. It showers individuals and Earth with cosmic abundance and when you are cosmically abundant, you are also abundant in your physical, mental, emotional and spiritual life. This energy enables you to connect with the wisdom of Golden Atlantis.

~ The Cosmic Crown Chakra ~

Curonay is the ascended aspect of Uranus and this has the vibration of divine transformation to a higher level and to bring enlightenment.

~ The Cosmic Causal Chakra ~

This is the Moon, a fully ascended chakra, which holds all the higher divine feminine qualities including compassion, love, togetherness, caring, empathy, nurturing and co-operation. It also has the ability to embrace a high and wide perspective of situations and to empower people to work as a cohesive whole.

~ The Cosmic Soul Star Chakra ~

Orion is seventh-dimensional, so it has no higher aspect. It holds cosmic wisdom.

~ The Cosmic Stellar Gateway Chakra ~

Nigellay is the ascended aspect of Mars. It uses its masculine energy to bring peace where it can and demonstrates the divine masculine qualities of the peaceful warrior, constructive action, strength with gentleness, inspirational leadership, the power to protect the weak and courage.

Chakra	Planet star or galaxy	Ascended seventh-dimensional aspect
Earth Star	Neptune	TOUTILLAY
Base	Saturn	QUISHY
Sacral	Sirius	LAKUMAY
Navel	Sun	SUN
Solar Plexus	Earth	PILCHAY
Heart	Venus	VENUS
Throat	Mercury	TELEPHONY
Third Eye	Jupiter	JUMBAY
Crown	Uranus	CURONAY
Causal	Moon	MOON
Soul Star	Orion	ORION
Stellar Gateway	Mars	NIGELLAY

When Kathy and I are receiving information I bring in the names. Kumeka spells them out to me telepathically one letter at a time. I say them aloud and write them down as he gives them to me, so I do not have the whole word until he has finished. I was completely fascinated by the names of the ascended aspects of the planets, especially for Mars, the Stellar Gateway, which is Nigellay, as I have a brother called Nigel. I asked if there was a connection and Kumeka replied that my brother came from Nigellay and was a highly evolved soul.

Also fascinating was Telephony, the higher aspect of Mercury, the planet of communication, the throat chakra. Whoever named the telephone was very psychically attuned! When we asked about Jumbay, the higher aspect of Jupiter, the third eye, we were told that it came from the vibration of hugeness and expansion, and immediately thought of Jumbo the elephant. Curonay, the ascended Uranus, is the coronet at the crown chakra.

I was also interested to see that the ascended aspects of the stars, planets and galaxies end in Y, which is the vibration of the angels. If someone has a Y in their name it connects them to the angelic realms. My middle name was chosen after my aunt Gwendy, who was christened Gwendoline. In my case my parents spelt it Gwendolyn, so my mother was clearly communicating telepathically with my soul when I was born; spelling my name with a Y undoubtedly helped my connection with the angels.

Some years ago when I wrote Discover Atlantis with Shaaron Hutton, I was given Lakuma as the ascended aspect of Sirius, the star from where horses and unicorns come. Now with our new awareness we asked why Lakuma did not end in Y. We were told it did. In full it is Lakumay but people were not ready for that vibration when the former books were written. Now the planet has risen in frequency and people are able to connect to Lakumay. The letter A brings in the divine feminine, so where the star, planet or galaxy ends in AY, it is balancing the yin and yang.

- **The KEY is to know that you are linked to all the stars, planets and galaxies.**

- **The SOUND is the hum of the divine cosmic flow.**

- **The COLOUR is silver and gold entwined.**

EXERCISE: *Visualization to align with the seventh-dimensional aspects of the cosmic chakras*

You can do this visualization in its entirety or you can focus on one chakra at a time.

1. Find a place where you can be quiet and undisturbed.
2. Light a candle if possible.
3. Relax and close your eyes.
4. Ground yourself by imagining roots going from you deep into the earth.
5. Place Archangel Michael's blue cloak of protection around you.
6. Focus on your Earth Star chakra and breathe in the energy of the Universal Angel Sandalphon. Then call in the light of Neptune and feel it entering your Earth Star. When you have completed this, take the frequency higher by invoking Toutillay. Allow yourself to relax and draw in the wisdom.
7. Repeat the above by focussing on your base chakra, breathing in the energy of Archangel Gabriel, then working with the light of Saturn and Quishy.
8. Repeat by focussing on your sacral chakra, working with Archangel Gabriel, Sirius and Lakumay.
9. Repeat by focussing on your navel chakra, working with Archangel Gabriel and the sun.
10. Repeat by focussing on your solar plexus chakra, working with Archangel Uriel, Earth and Pilchay.
11. Repeat by focussing on your heart chakra, working with Archangel Chamuel and Venus.
12. Repeat by focussing on your throat chakra, working with Archangel Michael, Mercury and Telephony.
13. Repeat by focussing on your third eye chakra, working with Archangel Raphael, Jupiter and Jumbay.

14. Repeat by focussing on your crown chakra, working with Archangel Jophiel, Uranus and Curonay.
15. Repeat by focussing on your causal chakra, working with Archangel Christiel and the moon.
16. Repeat by focussing on your soul star chakra, working with Archangel Mariel and Orion.
17. Repeat by focussing on your stellar gateway chakra, working with Archangel Metatron, Mars and Nigellay.
18. When you have drawn in the energy of the higher connections, relax and feel yourself as a being of the universe.
19. Then return to where you started and open your eyes.

EXERCISE: *To expand your fifth-dimensional chakras*

1. Find a large piece of paper and coloured pens.
2. Draw an outline of your body.
3. Colour in your twelve fifth-dimensional chakras.
4. Against each one write the seventh-dimensional name of the associated cosmic chakras.
5. As you do so sense the vibrational energy of the higher chakras.

The Nature Kingdom – The Elements

Everyone contains the four elements, air, water, earth and fire. Many people have a tendency to one or two of them and need to bring themselves into balance. When you are totally in balance you are one of the Keys to the universe. The qualities of the elements are linked to planets, stars or galaxies and in this chapter we offer you tools to access those you need.

It is easier for you to carry the qualities of your astrological birth sign and if you have several planets in one sign you may need to access the traits of the others in order to find equilibrium in your life.

> *For example I am a Virgo, which is Earth, and I have seven Earth planets in my chart, with no air and indeed I am very grounded but have to keep a balance of work and play. Kathy is a Capricorn, which is also Earth. She has three planets in Earth, three in water, four in air and two in fire so she is pretty balanced.*

~ AIR – the star system and qualities to which this element is connected ~

Air is connected to Lakumay, which is the ascended aspect of Sirius. This star holds certain qualities, which we can access through the element of air. These are enlightenment, ascension, enthusiasm, peace, purity, clear vision, high trust, the ability to access spiritual technology, courage, the ability to see a higher perspective, higher mental qualities such as the ability to see solutions or to see the divine vision, grace, dignity, inspired thoughts, empowering others, freedom, mental healing.

~ Breathing ~

The breath of life contains the essence of Source. As we breathe air in it enters our cells and brings light into them. The quality of breathing is important. The more deeply you breathe the more Source light you take in, which keeps you calm and peaceful and dissolves fear.

~ Breathing into the solar plexus ~

When you breathe in and out evenly from the solar plexus, this is known as a peace breath, for it puts you in contact with your deepest inner peace, which in turn allows you to access your inner wisdom.

Place your hands on your solar plexus and breathe comfortably in to the count of four and out to the count of four. Relax and feel yourself becoming more peaceful.

~ Breathing deeply into the abdomen ~

When you breathe deeply into your abdomen this enables you to take in the breath of life, which connects you with acceptance of nature, the angelic kingdom, unicorns, elementals, masters and the entire cosmos.

If you hum, cry or shout on the outbreath you dissolve negativity around you because the angels sing harmonics into the sound and help clear the space in your aura. This only happens if you are breathing into your abdomen but it is the reason why certain courses where you scream out your lower feelings are so helpful and transformational.

~ Pant breathing ~

Pant breathing puts you in touch with your blocked emotions and helps to bring them to the surface. In order to clear the emotion you need to follow this by breathing into your abdomen, making the sound of the feeling as you exhale. The angels will then transmute the old.

As we were receiving the above information about pant breathing one of the blinds in my conservatory suddenly unrolled and fell off so that we could see the sunny garden. Kumeka said, 'Now something has cleared in your knowledge.

Look how clearly you can see.' He really wanted us to understand the importance of pant and abdominal breathing with sound for dissolving stuck emotions.

~ Snoring ~

Snoring is caused by a blockage. This can have emotional reasons or can also be caused by eating the wrong food. It is an unconscious effort by the person to make the sounds that call in the angels, who will then make the sonics to heal them. At some level we are all questing to become whole.

Air carries energy. If you are in the mountains on a beautiful clear day you may, for example, feel the high frequency held by the air. The same applies to the oceans or to the forests where the trees have cleansed the energy. People are automatically drawn to these high vibration places and recognize that nature helps to create pure air.

Human thoughts affect the quality of the air around them. When your thoughts are pure the air is clear. Singing in harmony also clarifies it.

~ Air elementals and their role ~

When air moves, under the command of Dom, the Elemental Master of Air, it cleanses and raises the energy of everything it touches. The air elementals, the sylphs, assist with this. They work with flowers and plants, keeping the air round them pure and enabling the light of the sun to enter the leaves. The sylphs respond to the thoughts of humans and this affects the severity of the cleansing. If enough humans hold their thoughts calm and peaceful, we can transform a hurricane into a breeze.

Esaks are also air elementals, which gobble up and transmute lower energies, especially those left by humans.

Fairies too are of the element air and tend the flowers. They are about 1ft or 30 cms tall and are pure, innocent fun-loving beings. They help the angels and unicorns.

~ The Key to the element air ~

In order to absorb and have available to you more of the qualities of air that we list above take the following simple action. If you are out in nature attune to the fairies, connect to Lakumay, Sirius and breathe in the air qualities. If you are indoors call in the esaks, connect to Lakumay, Sirius, and breathe those higher traits. Wherever you are, but especially if you are out in a breeze or wind telepathically ask the sylphs to cleanse and clear your aura.

~ FIRE – the star system and qualities to which this element is connected ~

This element is connected to the higher aspect of Mars, Nigellay, which carries the following qualities that you can access for your own spiritual growth: Leadership by inspiring others, wise guidance, the ability to give freely and receive with gratitude, feel deserving, discipline, expressing yourself creatively, transmutation and release, celebration, ceremony, healing by transmuting emotions, delight, excitement, uncording and releasing, vitality, energy, radiant laughter.

~ Using the element of fire ~

Fire cleanses by breaking up lower energies and transmuting them to a higher frequency. When used correctly it is a wonderfully inspirational element. Sitting round a bonfire lifts people's spirits, and fireworks bring delight and celebration. Used with pure intent a lit candle for meditation spreads balance and harmony. Cooking over a fire adds spiritual energy to the food or water like a blessing.

When you light a fire it draws the fire qualities to you. And if you light a fire while holding the intent of drawing in those particular qualities it brings them in even more strongly.

~ Smudging with a sage stick ~

This is a way of cleansing a person or a space with the element of fire and air. Light the sage stick and waft it round someone's energy field. This also prepares their aura to accept the wisdom held in the sage. If you use any other kind of stick the energies of that herb will enter the field of the person.

~ Fire elementals and their role ~

The Elemental Master of Fire is Thor. His elementals are the salamanders and fire dragons.

When you call in the salamanders as you light a fire they will help you bring in the higher qualities of Nigellay, Mars, and develop them.

Dragons may be of air, earth or fire, while water dragons are really water serpents. They are fourth-dimensional elementals and apart from water serpents all have fire and carry its qualities, which they use to transmute the old and raise the frequency. You can call them in to help you when you are meditating, asleep, need protection or want to transmute the old. If you are under psychic attack they will actively intervene. They are wonderful, faithful companions and are especially helpful to look after sensitive children.

~ The Key to the element fire ~

The Key is to light a candle, connect to Nigellay, Mars, and draw in the fire qualities.

~ WATER – the planet and qualities to which this element is connected

Water is connected to the planet Neptune and these are the qualities held there that we can contact: flowing, cleansing, purifying, grace, healing, relaxation, peace, fulfillment, enlivening, dissolving the old, bringing higher dreams, bringing the feminine into balance, adding energy to a vision, nourishment, refreshment, bringing to life, life giving, clearing, enlightenment, satisfaction, clearing away old limitations, expansion, going with the flow, trusting the current of life, playfulness, wisdom, cosmic knowledge, serenity, intuition, psychism, clairaudience, clairvoyance, clairsentience, stellar connections.

Pure water contains cosmic cleansing and healing properties. If you bless all water and are grateful for it before you drink it or bathe in it, it will raise your frequency and enable you to absorb its divine essence.

~ Water elementals and their role ~

The Elemental Master of Water is Neptune and his elementals are kyhils, mermaids and undines.

Kyhils are tiny little beings that cleanse the waters of the rivers and oceans. Mermaids work predominantly with the flora and fauna of the oceans while undines help to keep the waters of the world pure and clear.

In any form of water, such as rain, snow, a bath, or the sea, breathe into Neptune and ask the elementals to help you absorb the qualities. Call on the kyhils if you are in rain or snow, the mermaids if you are swimming in a lake, river or ocean, the undines if you are in a bath or shower.

~ The Key to the element water ~

The Key is to relax in water and connect to Neptune, then call in the water qualities.

~ EARTH – the planet and qualities to which this element is connected ~

The element of earth is not surprisingly connected to our own planet and the qualities are: groundedness, common sense, capability, physical healing, reliability, sensible, cheerful, connected, loving, practical, dedicated, disciplined, inspired, leadership, good example, understanding properties of plants, crystals and soil for the higher good, ability to teach, comprehend concepts, honesty, trustworthiness, capable, confident, self-worth, abundant, fertile, accepting, ability to see expanded concepts, maternal, nurturing, wisdom, knowledge, giving and receiving in balance, ability to bring forward ancient wisdom, determination.

~ Earth elementals and their role ~

The Elemental Master of Earth is Taia and his elementals are goblins, warburtons and elves. Goblins and warburtons are fifth-dimensional and carry all the highest aspects of the earth qualities, connecting them to places and imparting them to people. They also bring fifth-dimensional people and places together.

> I was interested when Kumeka told us this for while I was in Findhorn I saw three goblins who live locally to me. They were with three Findhorn goblins and were very preoccupied. Later Gobolino told me that they were connecting the energy of my home with Findhorn.

Elves are fourth-dimensional and bring in the qualities at a fourth-dimensional level to those who are ready.

~ *The Key to the element of earth* ~

The Key is to go into nature, link to Hollow Earth through your Earth Star chakra and draw in the earth qualities.

■ **The KEY to the elements is to connect with earth, air, fire and water and bring the qualities they carry into perfect balance.**

■ **The SOUND is silence and stillness.**

■ **The COLOUR is white.**

EXERCISE: *Visualization to balance the elements within you*

1. Find a place where you can be quiet and undisturbed.
2. If possible light a candle to raise the vibration.
3. Close your eyes and relax.
4. Ground yourself by imagining roots growing from your feet deep down into the earth.
5. Place Archangel Michael's blue cloak of protection around you.
6. Visualize yourself on a hilltop on a breezy day. You can see for miles around you. Just relax into the beauty.
7. The air is clear and cool and you can feel the old being blown away from you.
8. With every in-breath you are drawing in the air qualities; they are being anchored and balanced in you.
9. You can see a fire being started below you at the edge of a lake and are inexorably drawn towards it.
10. Walk down the hill and approach the fire. You can see the bright sparks of the salamanders. They are showering all over you, filling your aura until eventually you are enfolded in a golden flame, which is burning away your dross.
11. Then you breathe in the qualities of fire and they are being anchored and balanced in you.
12. You walk to the edge of the beautiful, clear lake. You enjoy watching the ripples and the light on the surface.
13. Wade into the water until you can swim, float or just lie in it. As you relax in the lake bless the water so that it cleanses and purifies you.

14. Breathe in the wonderful qualities of the element water, knowing they are being anchored and balanced in you.
15. There is a grassy place by the lake and you move here to stretch out on the earth.
16. Feel the earth supporting you and drawing from you any toxins or stuck energy.
17. Breathe in the earth qualities and know they are being anchored and balanced in you.
18. Stand up and walk along the edge of the lake, aware that at this moment the elements in you are in total balance.
19. How does this feel? How differently do you perceive life? What decisions can you take from this balanced perspective? Treasure this feeling for a while.
20. When you are ready, return to the place from where you started and open your eyes.

EXERCISE: *To cleanse yourself through fire*

After meditation with a candle, cup your hands round it and draw the energy of it around your aura to cleanse it. This will also bring the higher qualities of the meditation into your electromagnetic field.

EXERCISE: *To balance your qualities of giving and receiving through fire*

For many evolved people this aspect needs to be balanced and this simple exercise will help you. Do it with intention and the fire will perform its magic to balance your qualities of giving and receiving.

1. Light a candle.
2. Write down everything you are grateful for.
3. Burn the paper.
4. This clears the imbalance of giving and receiving from your aura.

EXERCISE: *To balance the elements*

If you have your astrological birth chart, count how many planets you have in each of the elements of earth, air, fire and water. Pay particular attention to the ones you are short of and concentrate on bringing these qualities into your life and your aura.

Sacred Geometry

Shapes create a flow. Certain shapes alter vibrations in specific ways and can enhance the stream. The ancients did not question but accepted the currents and worked out the effects of the shape. Now with the advancement of science our programming is to question why and this is a third-dimensional example of how we put up barriers to natural movements.

> *When Kathy and I were in Guatemala we were walking around one of the Ancient Mayan sites. Suddenly our guide stood still and started talking about the stars and the alignment with the pyramids. He started to draw in the soil with a stick to explain to us. Imagine our excitement and amazement when he drew the Metatron Cube! This confirmed to us how connected the ancient Mayans were to sacred geometry.*

Flow is the natural breath of God.

~ The influence of the masculine and the feminine ~

The masculine force of the left-brain rationalizes, examines, defines scientifically and tries to prove God and God's energy. The feminine energy of the right brain has a natural flow of divine qualities, wisdom, compassion, love, joy, co-operation and peace. *Sacred geometry brings the feminine and masculine into perfect balance and harmony. For example, the symbol of the cross in a circle demonstrates ideal balance and harmony.*

Whether you sit in a square or a triangle it is important to accept what feels right for you. However, many people use their logical left-brain and question why a triangle should be right at that moment.

~ Buildings and gardens ~

Everything is divinely created with the exact balance of masculine and feminine. In the past when sacred buildings or gardens were created, the yin and yang were perfectly balanced and the people who lived or worked within them were influenced by this harmony.

We can change sick building syndrome into harmonious building syndrome by using sacred geometry.

~ Our bodies ~

Every cell in our bodies contains sacred geometry, with a balance of masculine and feminine.

~ The twelve chakras ~

Each shape aligns with a colour, chakra and archangel.

Chakra	Shape	Colour	Archangel
Earth Star	Circle	Black and white	Sandalphon
Base	Square	Platinum	Gabriel
Sacral	Oval	Pale pink	Gabriel
Navel	Oval	Orange	Gabriel
Solar Plexus	Six-pointed star	Gold	Uriel
Heart	Yin yang symbol	White	Chamuel
Throat	Upward triangle	Royal blue	Michael
Third Eye	Figure of eight	Transparent	Raphael
Crown	Open or closed pyramid	Transparent	Jophiel
Causal	A cone with spiralling energy going out into the universe and coming back in	White	Christiel
Soul Star	Five-pointed star	Magenta	Mariel
Stellar Gateway	The cosmic Metatron Cube	Gold	Metatron

~ *Sacred Geometric Shapes* ~

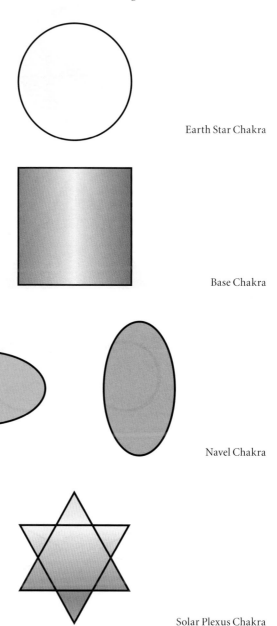

Earth Star Chakra

Base Chakra

Sacral Chakra

Navel Chakra

Solar Plexus Chakra

Heart Chakra

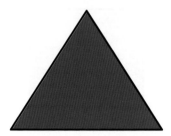

Throat Chakra

Third Eye Chakra

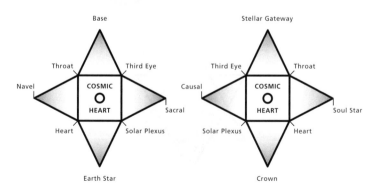

Crown Chakra

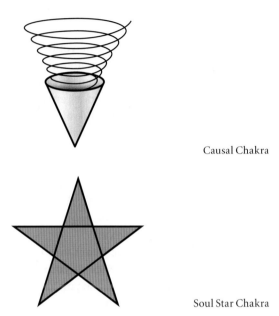

Causal Chakra

Soul Star Chakra

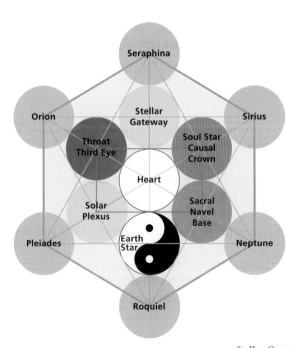

Stellar Gateway Chakra

~ *The Cosmic Heart* ~

The cosmic heart is the chakra of Venus and it connects through the cosmic heart of our planet in Guatemala right into the centre of Hollow Earth, and then radiates its energy out through the ley lines. It is the heartbeat of the universe and its energy is held by Source. Mother Mary, the unicorns, Seraphina, Butyalil, Metatron and the energy of all the planets link into the cosmic heart.

If you imagine yourself sitting in the centre of a tetrahedron in the cosmic heart of the universe, you will receive light from all the stars, planets and galaxies. You become more than a being on this planet. You take your place as a Cosmic Being. A part of you is then linked to the seventh dimension. The cosmic heart is golden with petals linking to all the stars, planets and galaxies.

When you sit in the cosmic heart you link to your original divine spark, your Monad, the essence of your being. At that moment you are seventh-dimensional because you are going with the cosmic flow. Sacred geometry facilitates this.

■   **The KEY is to understand and trust the divine in all things.**

■   **The SOUND is that of water lapping.**

■   **The COLOUR is orange.**

EXERCISE: *Visualization to energize the stars, planets and galaxies through sacred geometry*

1. Find a place where you can be quiet and undisturbed.
2. Light a candle if possible.
3. Relax and close your eyes.
4. Ground yourself by imagining roots going from you deep into the earth.
5. Place Archangel Michael's blue cloak of protection around you.
6. Picture energy coming up from Hollow Earth through each of the sacred geometric shapes into each of your chakras in turn, each facilitating the flow to the next one until you reach the Stellar Gateway.
7. Then let it flow into the Cosmic Heart.

8. From here draw energy and send it to all the stars, planets and galaxies. Take plenty of time for this.
9. When you have finished, come back to your present reality and open your eyes.

EXERCISE: *To connect with the sacred geometry*

1. Create the geometric shapes or at least two or three of them with chalk, stones or string.
2. Sit in each one for a time and notice what you feel.

EXERCISE: *To draw sacred geometric shapes*

1. Draw the shapes separately or overlapping and colour them in.
2. As you do so reflect on the sacred geometry of the universe.

Light

There are many different frequencies of light and all contain varying levels of spiritual information and knowledge. Fast-frequency light contains higher wisdom.

Light is not necessarily visible to us. We can only see it up to the fourth-dimensional frequency. Light beyond the fourth-dimension penetrates our cells with spiritual knowing but we are not necessarily aware of it.

You can be in a dark room and be able to 'see' everything, though not physically. You can be in a sun-filled meadow and 'see' nothing. The light of spiritual illumination is about consciousness.

Your light is the energy of your soul or your divine spark radiating through you. Then you are illuminated with joy, clarity, love, wisdom, knowledge and other wonderful qualities and feelings. Light is a feature of the frequency of your cells.

Your light is seen as your aura, the electromagnetic field around you.

~ *Third-dimensional aura* ~

A third-dimensional person is holding their cells closed because they are grasping things only for themselves. Their aura is quite near to their body and the colours may be dull. This may result in illness until they are ready to expand.

However, there are many reasons for illness, so it may not be indicative of being a third-dimensional being. Because this is the end of an era, all things of a lower nature are coming to the surface to be cleansed and this often manifests as disease. You may be holding onto something from your past in this life or a previous one. Some people are ill because they are clearing lower energy for everyone. If you are doing ancestral release work or healing of the collective consciousness, this is a soul choice. Another reason for disease is that your soul may desperately want to learn something from an illness.

Many souls who are of higher dimensions hold a great deal of light but they are out of balance. For example their masculine and feminine or their emotional and mental bodies might be out of kilter and this causes problems in their physical bodies.

We were asked to write about teenagers in this chapter as society is currently creating third-dimensional adults by restricting them in their adolescence. Many youngsters are trying to follow their hearts, which is the only way to become a glorious divine being, but we are not empowering them to do this. Instead we restrict them with rules. 'You will not play music and be creative. You will study mathematics and history.' 'There is no money in travelling the world. You have got to pass your exams.' 'You have got to go to school every day even though it does not suit your personality and will not equip you for your future.' Instead of trying to understand and work with our regulations, because of their physiological changes, teenagers resist them and become stuck. We expect them to act like young adults but they do not know who they are and often go off track.

The teenage years are critical for they either remain stuck in the third dimension or they emerge on their paths. We need to provide an environment where they can blossom into their own individuality.

~ Fourth-dimensional aura ~

Your aura is expanding because you feel safer to let people in. You are happy to share more of your light.

~ Fifth-dimensional aura ~

Now you have no secrets so you have nothing to lock away. You have a widely expanded aura that embraces and includes others. You consciously spread your light to others and are happy to receive from them.

~ Clairaudience ~

When your throat chakra is illuminated with light you become clairaudient. You hear or receive telepathically the thoughts of other people or the spirit world and angels.

~ Clairsentience ~

When your sacral and navel chakras are illuminated with light you become clairsentient, in other words you feel the feelings of others.

~ Clairvoyance ~

When your third eye is illuminated with light you become clairvoyant. You see with your inner eye through the veils into other dimensions.

~ Soul Star Chakra ~

This contains seventh-dimensional light. Hugely expanded understanding and wisdom now filters through from this chakra and illuminates your aura more.

~ Stellar Gateway Chakra ~

This contains the frequency of your Monad. The purest understanding and wisdom filters into your aura from this chakra and fills it with divine light. People who cannot see or hear psychically can feel the auras around people, in other words they can touch the light. So if someone vibrates with love, joy, laughter, wisdom, peace and other higher qualities, you can sense this by feeling their aura.

■ **The KEY is to consciously expand your aura at all times.**

■ **The SOUND is that of a cosmic harmony.**

■ **The COLOUR is white-blue.**

EXERCISE: *Visualization to expand your fifth-dimensional aura*

1. Find a place where you can be quiet and undisturbed.
2. If possible raise the vibration by lighting a candle.
3. Relax and close your eyes.
4. Ground yourself by imagining roots going from you deep into the earth.
5. Place Archangel Michael's blue cloak around you.

6. Send love, joy, peace, healing, wisdom, happiness and other high quality energies out into your aura.
7. Imagine the beautiful colours swirling around you.
8. Sense your aura expanding as you open up more and more.
9. See any secrets as blotches that are now fading away as they are exposed to the light of day. There is nothing to hide and you are safe.
10. Imagine yourself at work, at home, with your friends or in any other place with your aura open wide.
11. Embrace others in your wonderful fifth-dimensional aura. Notice how you feel and how they feel.
12. Let the angels pour light and love into you, lighting you up even more.
13. When you are ready, thank the angels, open your eyes, enjoy your full expansion and return to your current physical space.

The more frequently you do this, the bigger and more beautiful your aura will become. If you wish to you can consciously expand your aura as you live your daily life but remember to put a protection around yourself.

EXERCISE: *To feel the light of someone's aura*

Find someone or several people who are willing to let you feel the light of their auras. Ask one to sit on a chair sideways, so that you can feel the energy round their back. Alternatively they can lie on the floor.

1. Ground yourself by feeling the floor firmly underneath your body.
2. Place Archangel Michael's cloak of protection around yourself and the other person.
3. Tune into the person you are working with by breathing the energy from their heart into yours or by placing your hands on their shoulders.
4. Ask the angels to assist you for your highest good and the highest good of the friend you are working with.
5. Rub your hands together to activate the energy.
6. With your palms open move your hands towards them until you can feel a tingle or a resistance, which indicates the edge of their aura. Now run your hands around their aura.
7. You might like to close your eyes and sense the colour, the qualities

and the spiritual information contained within the aura.

8. When you have finished, mentally disconnect your energy from that of the friend you were working with.
9. Thank the angels and your friend.
10. If appropriate share with your friend what you felt. And discover what they felt as you did this.

EXERCISE: *To sense the light of someone's aura*

This is an intuitive drawing exercise, so you will need paper and crayons or felt tips. You will also require someone who is happy to let you draw their aura. Let them sit in front of you, preferably in front of a white wall though this is not essential.

1. Ground yourself by feeling the floor firmly underneath your body.
2. Place Archangel Michael's cloak of protection around yourself.
3. Tune into the person you are working with by breathing the energy from their heart into yours.
4. Ask the angels to help you for your highest good and the highest good of the person you are working with.
5. You may like to draw a circle or shape to indicate their head.
6. Do not think about it but intuitively choose colours that you sense in your friend's aura.
7. As you crayon or colour, let the angels guide you.
8. When you have finished mentally disconnect your energy from your friend.
9. Thank the angels and your friend.
10. Discuss the aura you have drawn, the information it contains and how you both feel.

Sonic Sounds

Sound is third-dimensional. When the angels add their energy to sound it becomes a fast-frequency sonic emitted for specific high-vibrational purposes. We may not be able to hear it because it is beyond our auditory range and our understanding of it is limited but it has a powerful effect.

Sonics are angelic harmonies that respond to love, sacred geometry, pure intention and peace breathed in alignment with the breath of God.

~ Thunder ~

Thunder breaks up the accumulation of lower energies in the atmosphere. It shatters negativity, which has been blown into an area so that those below do not receive it. Sheet lightening is the physical manifestation of the transmutation. Fork lightening brings the positive transmuted energy down to the ley lines to be spread through the planet.

~ Sonic of the dolphins ~

This clears the path in front of the dolphins of lower frequencies so that they can find their direction through pure energies. Water is a cosmic element that contains the wisdom of the universe. When the frequency of the water is raised by the sonics, the dolphins can access and maintain the wisdom of Golden Atlantis.

~ Sonics for buildings ~

Certain perfect notes change the properties of matter. In former times specific notes chanted by spiritual people lightened stones. Then the stones could be moved by mind control to the envisioned place of construction. Sacred buildings were erected by this method. The buildings in the Golden Era of Atlantis were all created in this way.

~ The sound that shatters glass ~

This sound breaks up constructs that are no longer for the highest good.

~ Levitation ~

Levitation can be effected without human sound but as you hold the intention to lift someone, the angels make the sounds, which lighten the matter of the person being raised. Then they rise without any support.

~ Becoming invisible ~

Like levitation you do not need sound to become invisible. When you raise your frequency to become one with your surroundings, the angels attune you to them so that you are no longer visible.

Many years ago I was sitting on a bench in the garden of a special spiritual community. I felt at total peace. When my group came to find me, they were looking at me and could not see me. Then I came back to Earth and reappeared, rather to their surprise!

~ Teleporting ~

In order to teleport your physical body so that you disappear and appear somewhere else, the angels change the frequency of your cells. This was quite a common gift in the Golden Era of Atlantis.

~ Sonics that help plants and trees to grow ~

When you open your heart and talk, mentally or aloud, to plants and trees, the angels send sonics to help them grow.

~ Elementals work with plants ~

The elementals, such as fairies and elves, hold the vision of the blue-print of the plant and the angels make the sonics to help it fulfil its potential.

~ A buzz or sharp pain in your ear ~

When you hear a buzz or even feel a sharp pain in your ear, your angels and guides are breaking down your resistance and trying to raise your frequency.

> Both Kathy and I have experienced this many times. Archangel Metatron buzzes my right ear or inflicts a sudden twinge in it when he wants to draw attention to something. I know immediately that I have to pay attention, ground myself or think of something more positively. Kumeka and occasionally other guides or angels do the same in my left ear.
>
> Kathy finds that, if she is still not listening after all other nudges from the angelic realms, such as a feeling or an ache in her third eye, they will buzz her ears.

~ Sacred geometry and sonics ~

When a building is designed according to sacred geometry the angels sing the sonics to bring it to completion in a perfect divine way. The cathedral of Sacre Coeur in France is an example of this, as is Salisbury Cathedral, which has been built on a flood plain so the water is keeping the energy pure. Angels do not offer sonics to haphazardly created constructions.

A pyramid that is perfectly aligned to the ascension planets, stars and galaxies attracts amazing harmonics which people can feel as they enter it.

~ Healing ~

The angels respond with sonics to the vision of divine perfection held by the healer and the person being healed.

~ Mother and baby ~

When a mother opens her heart and sings or hums to her baby, the angels add their energy through sonics to strengthen the bond of love between them.

~ The moon ~

Angels sing over the world at full moon and the sonics enter the waters to purify them and raise their frequency. The sonics do not move the water.

~ The elements ~

In a magnificent place in nature where there are the elements of fire (sun), air (gentle breeze), earth (glorious vegetation) and water (snow, stream, lake or sea), the angels will sing sonics over that area and raise the frequency even more. This is why certain beauty spots touch us so deeply.

~ The dawn chorus ~

The angels make harmonics through the singing birds, which are raising the frequency of humans, animals and the whole of nature.

~ Singing bowls ~

Singing bowls make perfect vibrations for angels to work through to clear stuck energy.

Rosemary Stephenson is one of the teachers of the Diana Cooper School and a good friend of mine. She takes her crystal bowls everywhere she goes. I have been with her in diverse places such as the crypt of Rosslyn Chapel in Scotland, Angkor Wat Temples in Cambodia and an igloo in the Arctic where she has sung with her bowls. The sound is angelic and you can hear the angels responding and transforming the energy. Rosemary also plays her singing bowls at seminars and for CDs. You can feel and hear the presence of angels.

~ Music ~

When music is played, whatever the instrument, with high pure intention for the greatest good, the angels create harmonics. The intention of the listener also affects this.

> My friend Diane Egby Edwards plays every instrument possible including the gong, the didgeridoo, flutes and crystal bowls. She finds that the acoustics in my kitchen are ideal for the didgeridoo and the angels love it too.
> Kathy finds that there is a particular song that pulls her heartstrings. She knows that when it is played the angels sing over her to break up old pain in her heart.

~ Our planet ~

There is much disharmony within our planet, which is making a roar like a runaway train. We are asked to envision Earth's perfection and ask the angels to sing harmonics over us until the planet emits a peaceful, loving purr.

Pure joyous laughter, the gentle wind in the trees, wind chimes, a waterfall, gentle waves, beautiful singing or the flap of a bird's wing are sonics that break up lower energies.

■ **The KEY is to do everything with the purest intention.**

■ **The SOUND is that of angels singing.**

■ **The COLOUR is pale yellow gold.**

EXERCISE: *Visualization to heal with harmonics*

1. Find a place where you can be quiet and undisturbed.
2. Light a candle if possible.
3. Relax and close your eyes.
4. Ground yourself by imagining roots going from your feet deep down into the earth.
5. Place Archangel Michael's blue cloak around you.
6. Hold the intention of healing someone for the highest good.

7. Picture them in total health.
8. You may like to hum as you ask the angels to sing over the person.
9. Imagine a cascade of beautiful harmonics showering over them.
10. Let go of any expectations. Just know you have done your part.
11. Thank the angels, return to the here and now and open your eyes.

EXERCISE: *Visualization for the divine perfection of the planet*

1. You can do this anywhere, inside or out, sitting, lying or walking.
2. Picture Earth as beautiful and with a wonderful glowing aura.
3. See all the animals, birds, trees, plants and humans singing together in perfect harmony.
4. Ask the angels to pour their harmonics over the world.
5. Sense the Earth purring or softly humming.
6. When you are finished, if they were closed, open your eyes.

EXERCISE: *Bathing in sound for the highest good*

1. Set your intention for the highest good.
2. Listen to a piece of music or play singing bowls.
3. Be aware of the angels singing with you.

Qualities for
Golden Earth

There are many qualities that unlock the doors to oneness. Each of these vibrates to a musical note and sacred geometric symbol. Together they create a symphony of truly magical powers. When this symphony is played and you open your heart to it, you feel and know true enlightenment. You are then in touch with the heartbeat of the Earth.

It is not enough to know intellectually about a quality. You have to feel it, explore it and incorporate it into your life. We were given twenty energies to explore for this Key and each one energetically creates a sacred geometric shape.

1.
~ Innocence, purity and unconditional
cosmic love – the infinity sign ~

Pure water is one medium through which divine love is spread and it holds these qualities.

2.
~ Humility and self-healing – circle ~

To understand true humility we were asked to think of a worm working quietly and humbly in the soil. Worms are hermaphrodite, so they reproduce themselves. If they are broken they can regenerate themselves. This gives us a symbolic vision of self-healing. One of the Keys is about self-healing, which includes self-responsibility and not blaming others. To be completely independent and aware you must be self-contained, in charge of who you are. Worms dedicate themselves to their work. They cannot see. They have to do it all by sensing. They offer us lessons in humility, self-reliance and dedication.

3.
~ Togetherness – circle ~

Without stars there would be no Earth. We are one celestial body, so it would be like a human body without a foot. They all have different energies and each one is essential for the others. Every living thing on this planet is infused with light from the stars, light that brings us spiritual information and knowledge and holds us together. Take time to look at the stars and feel our oneness.

4.
~ Learning – square ~

Wolves work together as a pack. Each has its recognized role within the group decided before birth and reflected in the order of birth. They learn from the wisdom of the elders to do what is perfect for the whole. As you contemplate this quality remember the wisdom of the wise ancients and how they worked together to honour the Earth and all on her.

5.
~ Joy of freedom, listening to divine messages, being adaptable – figure of eight ~

Have you ever watched a bird soaring through the sky and floating effortlessly on the air currents? They demonstrate the joy of freedom and have learnt to adapt themselves to work with the elements, especially air, using its flow. Have you heard one singing its heart out on a bush, reminding you to be happy whatever the conditions and to communicate it to the world? Birds listen to the message of the elements and teach us to live lightly. When you sit and watch the birds you learn invaluable messages.

6.
~ Intuition – figure of eight ~

There are times when we have to focus on our vision and go for it, following our inner knowing with determination. You can admire the courage and energy of salmon, which are driven by their instinct and their intuition. They know they must go against the flow to do what is right for them and they do it. Many creatures would give up in the face of such challenges to return to their spawning grounds but these fish simply trust.

7.
~ Grounded – square ~

Trees are the most gracious of sentient beings. They root themselves into the energy of the Earth and draw their sustenance from it, feeling its love and support. They follow their divine blueprint automatically and grow round or through obstacles without question always aiming for the light. They also hold and spread the wisdom of the ages. When you lean against a big tree you can feel the love from the Earth pulsing through it. It reminds you to anchor your feet in the ground and at the same time reach for the highest. You then become part of the cosmic web of light.

8.
~ Sacrifice and sweetness – open and closed pyramid ~

When you give up your life for another, perhaps by unconditionally looking after them, you offer divine grace and in doing so make your-self sacred. If at the same time you serve the universe by freely offer-ing sweetness to others, you become blessed. The greatest example of these qualities in action is demonstrated by bees, which live an ordered life and will sacrifice themselves for the good of the whole. At the same time they offer their sweetness and healing to other species. When you tune into these creatures and learn to understand them, you start to integrate their qualities.

9.
~ Wisdom with joy – figure of eight ~

The creatures on our planet that live joyfully, while holding the wis-dom of the universe are the dolphins. They are the High Priests and Priestesses of the oceans, protecting the weak and vulnerable, healing their own and other species and doing everything for the highest good of all. They have an ability to see the beauty in everyone and let them know they see it. Furthermore they communicate subliminally with others so that they feel enfolded and inspire loyalty from their own and other species, including humans. When you practise these qualities you become a High Priest or Priestess.

10.
~ Fire – oval ~

Fire is special. It raises the light, cleanses and relaxes people and allows them to attain a higher consciousness. It offers life giving warmth and welcome, giving people hope and most importantly, it enables people to see. When you seek these qualities within yourself and offer yourself to others, you are a giver of life.

11.
~ Beauty – six-pointed star ~

You only have to look at flowers with their radiant colours and innocent beauty to feel inspired. They teach us to respond to the light of the sun, which is the divine masculine so that we are automatically sustained by its life enhancing qualities. Flowers are in tune with the flow of the cosmos and when we do the same our inner beauty glows.

12.
~ The divine masculine – six-pointed star ~

On a sunny day everything feels happier, friendlier, lighter and brighter. The sun demonstrates the divine masculine. Its power and strength is life-giving and offers warmth and light to the world. When you bathe in the energy of the sun or visualize it and breathe it in you enhance your divine masculine energy.

13.
~ The divine feminine – five-pointed star ~

There is little more beautiful and mysterious than the moon. By gently radiating the divine feminine, it affects the tides, the wind and weather and keeps everything moving and flowing. When you bathe in the moonlight or visualize it and breathe it in, you enhance your divine feminine qualities.

14.
~ A newborn – yin yang ~

Most people are touched at a deep heart level when they see or hold a newborn, whether a baby or an animal for they feel its wisdom, innocence, harmlessness and vulnerability as it is still connected to the purity of Source. The fragility of the newborn puts us in touch with our own divine essence.

15.
~ Laughter – upward triangle ~

If you have ever watched a baby chuckling with pleasure or a horse galloping freely with its mane flying in the wind or a child sledging down a slope you have probably smiled or laughed with them. When someone laughs for the sheer joy and delight of being, they are at one with the joy and support of the universe. They are giving themselves unconditionally to life.

16.
~ Deep appreciation and gratitude for being alive – upward triangle ~

When you walk in bare feet in the dewy grass bathed in early morning sunshine, the world around you is fresh and clean and your heart bursts with the sheer wonder of being alive. That is gratitude. Each time you truly appreciate the wondrous world in which we live, you activate a response from the universe.

17.
~ Peace – cosmic Metatron Cube ~

Imagine a beloved and well-fed cat stretched out in the sun and sense its peace. When you are at one with yourself and the cosmos you are harmonized and harmless. Then you know that all is divinely perfect in your world and you experience the peace that passeth all understanding.

18.
~ Magic and mystery – five-pointed star ~

Have you seen the face of a toddler watching a butterfly emerge from a cocoon? It reminds you of the excitement of exploring the hidden wonders of the universe and knowing there is so much more to discover than that which you can see and touch. You may have felt it the first time you connected with a unicorn, an angel or a fairy or saw a shooting star or experienced a new dimension. There is always another realm of wonder waiting for you.

19.
~ Promise – cone with spiralling energy ~

Since time began humans have recognized the magic of a rainbow. It offers a promise from the universe that there are new and better things to come. It holds out hope and a positive knowing that the universe will now respond to the wishes and intentions of your heart and that all is happening in divine right order. Notice how you feel when you next see a rainbow for your heart's leap of delight is opening doors.

20.
~ Being in touch with the heartbeat
of the Earth – yin yang symbol ~

As we recognize the higher qualities in our daily lives, we start to attune to and feel the heartbeat of the Earth. Each quality vibrates on a different note and these sound together to create a harmonic or key. Being in touch with the heartbeat of the Earth is one of the Keys to the universe.

■ **The KEY is to treat yourself and others as a perfect divine being.**

■ **THE SOUND is that of an angelic harp.**

■ **The COLOUR is black and white, the yin and yang symbol.**

EXERCISE: *Visualization to experience the qualities of Golden Earth*

1. Decide which quality or shape you wish to explore.
2. Find a place where you can be quiet and undisturbed.
3. Light a candle if possible.
4. Relax and close your eyes.
5. Ground yourself by imagining roots growing from your feet deep into the earth.
6. Place Archangel Michael's blue cloak around you for protection.
7. Visualize the shape you have chosen and imagine you are sitting in it.
8. Connect with the corresponding golden quality within yourself and experience it fully.
9. Breathe it into your cells.
10. When you have finished, bring your awareness back to waking reality and open your eyes.
11. Practise that quality in your life.

EXERCISE: *To attune to the qualities of oneness*

Draw the shapes as you contemplate the qualities.
You can draw several and let them merge as you consider the energies they represent.

The Cosmic Heart

The cosmic heart energizes the crystal pyramids that formed the dome over Golden Atlantis. After the fall of Atlantis some of the pyramids were moved to strategic positions over portals on Earth, for example Mount Shasta, Uluru and the six cosmic pyramids, Egypt, Tibet, Greece, Mesopotamia, Peru and the Mayan one in South America. Others remained in the inner planes.

The Harmonic Convergence in 1987 marked the start of a twenty-five-year period of purification. At that time millions of people meditated and prayed for world peace and there was a huge response from the spiritual realms. St. Germain took the prayers to Source and the violet flame, which had always been used by the few, was returned for the utilization of the masses for the first time since the fall of Atlantis.

Another result of humanity's prayers was that the remainder of the crystal pyramids from the Dome were moved and spread throughout the universe. They are connected to each other by pure love and are waiting to be switched on in preparation for 2012.

As the spiritual heart chakra of the planet opens in Glastonbury in 2012 it will connect to the cosmic heart and this will ignite all the pyramids. Then the heart centres of all the planets, stars and galaxies in this universe will connect.

When they are all linked, the pyramids will swivel and join their energy to that of the Great Crystal Pyramid in Hollow Earth. Through sharing their wisdom, they will wake up the wisdom in the pyramid in Hollow Earth and they will all share their energy, wisdom and love. They will merge their divine essence and it will be spread by the cosmic quality of water. This will happen by 2032 and bring our universe fully into the fifth dimension.

The Pyramid of Hollow Earth will fully awaken and send the wisdom, energy and love down the ley lines. As we ground our Earth Star chakras we can connect with it. This will dramatically expand the consciousness of people by 2032 and break down all barriers to interstellar communication.

When you are ready you are taken to the cosmic heart by Mother Mary's angels to be enfolded in love.

■ **The KEY is to ask the angels to conduct your spirit in your sleep to the cosmic heart and enfold your spirit.**

■ **The SOUND is that of a baby when it is receiving love.**

■ **The COLOUR is gold, white and pink.**

EXERCISE: *Visualization to enter the cosmic heart*

1. Find a place where you can be quiet and undisturbed.
2. Raise the vibration by lighting a candle, if possible, or placing some flowers.
3. Relax and close your eyes.
4. Ground yourself by imagining roots going from you deep into the earth.
5. Place Archangel Michael's blue protective cloak around you.
6. Mother Mary and her angels are surrounding you and you can feel their wonderful compassion and love.
7. They are taking you to sit in the centre of a white and pink rose with a golden centre.
8. Feel the energy of pure love pouring into you.
9. A shimmering crystal pyramid is being placed over you.
10. Relax and enjoy the experience.
11. When it is time to return, Mother Mary and her angels collect you and take you back to where you started.
12. Gently open your eyes again.

EXERCISE: *To connect to the cosmic heart*

1. Draw a pink rose with a golden centre.
2 Place an image or photograph of yourself in it.
3. Draw a pyramid shape round the rose.

Pure Love –
Divine Connection

When Source sent out the original divine sparks which became Monads, they were made with pure love. Pure love is totally undemanding and accepting. It extends its energy to everything but you only feel it when you are in the moment.

Whenever you give or receive pure love the angels step in and pour their light through you.

~ Being in the moment ~

It is said that the NOW is a gift. It is 'the present'. When you are in the NOW you can receive pure love from people, the angels or the universe. The most perfect present!

~ Examples ~

If you are in shock after an accident and people are looking after you with compassion, their love enters all your chakras and lights you up at a cellular level. It is a very pure form of healing because the shock opens you up to accept it.

During times of total stillness and acceptance, such as when you are in meditation or watching a glorious sunset, angels, unicorns or elementals can touch you with pure love which affects the cells of your body.

If you are having fun or laughing uproariously with delight the angels, elementals, unicorns or any being of the spiritual realms can touch you.

When you are in contact with the elements, air, water, fire or earth the spiritual realms can pour pure love into you more easily. This includes if you are floating in the sea or are relaxing in the sun, when you are dancing in the wind, walking barefoot in earth, staring into the flames of a fire or lying on the earth watching a bee or a flower. The realms of spirit can use these times to pour divine love into you.

Some people experience this when they are swimming with the dolphins. If you let go of your fear of the water and your concentration on swimming, so that you are just in the moment, the dolphins will bring you the pure love of the angels.

As he was telling us this, my guide, Kumeka asked us to think of times when we had felt this connection.

Kathy had a bliss moment when she was at Durlston Head, Dorset, England. With bare feet in the long grass, she was looking over the ocean, with the sun on her back and the wind blowing in her hair. She was looking for dolphins and though she could not see them apparently they were there. At that moment the angels were touching her.

When you are with the big animals and their majestic energy, power, strength and lack of fear fill you with awe in those moments, you can receive pure love from the angels. When I was in Kenya many years ago doing a dawn walk with a guide, we passed through giraffes, elephants and other big game. I felt a marvellous sense of peace and awe and that was one such magical moment in my life when the angels touched me, though I was not aware of it at that time.

On another occasion I was visiting my son and his partner who were in New Zealand for a year. For Christmas they bought me one of the best presents of my life – a day out whale watching. We saw hundreds of whales diving around our boat; all flipping their huge tails and it was simply magical. The angels touched us.
Similarly when I sat on the sandy floor of a canyon in Thailand and held a huge tiger's head on my lap. As I telepathically connected with the tiger and it responded to me, that was a bliss moment. So was the breath-catching moment in Hawaii when watching red molten lava stream into the ocean and another one when looking into the Grand Canyon. These are the spaces of such wonder that we allow the veils to

lift and the higher realms to connect with us. In those instants
magical and miraculous things can occur.

Moments of being in the now are often instants of crisis when you are in survival mode. For example if you are driving along a country road when a deer dashes across the road right in front of you, in the seconds when you slam on the brakes you receive a download of pure love to counterbalance the fear.

Kathy was on an aerial walkway in South America up a very
tall, wobbly, jungle tree (her description), when she felt a rush
of vertigo. We were told that at that instant she received from
the angels a surge of pure love and this helped her.

One of my daughters had meningitis at the age of ten weeks.
When I picked her up from her cradle I knew she was desper-
ately ill. I carried her on cotton wool legs downstairs to phone
the doctor. The angels said that at that moment they were
filling me with their love, strengthening me.

~ Being selfless ~

Pure cosmic love is poured into you when you remove yourself from the equation and become selfless. Soldiers who dash forward to save their comrades with no thought for their own safety receive this pure love in the form of courage from the angels. Even if they die in the attempt the angelic force is with them.

If you see an accident and rush to help the injured with no thought for your own life, the angels are pouring their energy into you. Pure angel love is the strength that enables a mother to raise a cupboard off her child that she could not normally lift. It provides a superhuman force.

Empowering others in any way is a form of pure love in which the angels assist you.

When you are selflessly helping nature you receive this love, for example if you are cleaning up a river and your only thought is for the animals and the water. If you are hurrying an injured animal to the vet with compassion, the angels come in to help you.

Those who are giving healing with their hearts open and the highest intent receive pure love, as do doctors, surgeons or nurses who work with a similar pure heart and mind focus.

When you selflessly ask that your spirit go out into the inner planes to help others while you sleep, this is an unconditional offer, which receives a response from the universe. Your spontaneous reaction to the needs of others or your attitude of caring are the energies that call in the higher forces to fill you with light.

~ Creativity ~

Passion and creativity are energies of pure love when poured into art, sculptures, gardens, music or any form of vision. The angels infuse their energy into the piece of work so that people can receive the divine love.

■ **The KEY to receiving is being in the moment and it opens you to a flow of angelic love. When you give from the heart the angels can step in and add their energy.**

■ **The SOUND is that of the heart beating.**

■ **The COLOUR is aquamarine for receiving, rose pink for giving.**

EXERCISE: *Visualization to give and to receive*

1. Find a place where you can be quiet and undisturbed.
2. Light a candle if possible.
3. Relax and close your eyes.
4. Ground yourself by imagining roots going from you deep into the earth.
5. Place Archangel Michael's blue cloak around you.
6. Surround yourself in rose pink love and visualize yourself giving to others from your heart.
7. Surround yourself in aquamarine and imagine yourself receiving with gratitude from others and the universe.
8. When you are finished, return your awareness to the room and open your eyes.

EXERCISE: *To practise giving from the heart*

Do something selfless today, for example spend time with someone who is lonely, listen without judgement, cook a friend their favourite meal. You can do anything. The most important part of this exercise is the openhearted way in which you do it without expectation of return.

EXERCISE: *To become aware of the present moment*

Practise living in the now today. In order to do this you must be constantly aware of your thoughts and feelings. Experience the feeling of every moment without thinking of the past or the future. It is helpful to say or think to yourself, 'At this moment I am......'

The Spiritual Laws
(Alchemy and Magic)

At a fifth-dimensional level the Law of Karma means that if you are given a lesson you must learn it and do something about it in a positive way. Then alchemical changes can take place.

Miracles are the result of bringing your energy or someone else's into alignment with divine perfection.

What you give out you receive back. For example positive thoughts are fifth-dimensional. They touch other people and raise their frequency, allowing a miraculous change of attitude to happen.

A couple I knew called George and Lorraine belonged to a club where there was a very unpopular member. He was always surly and grumbled about everything, so people tended to avoid him. George and Lorraine decided to send him only positive, loving thoughts and treat him as if they really liked him. They greeted him cheerfully when they met him, invited him to join them and focussed on his good qualities when they were thinking about him. He changed dramatically towards them, becoming friendly, relaxed and interesting. And before long he extended his new attitude towards the other members and is now a popular and welcome personality in the club.

~ Massage ~

If you are giving someone a massage while envisioning their divine perfection, there will be a deep cellular relaxation, which will promote a balanced flow of energy through the chakras. This can result in a magical shift in energy, health and attitude for your friend or client.

~ Psychic readings ~

When you do a spiritual or psychic reading with the positive intention of bringing forward information for the highest good of the person you are working with, you will access pure guidance for them.

~ Healing ~

Always focus on the divine perfection of the person to whom you are giving or sending healing. Your positive energy will bring it about if the patient is also in alignment with your vision. Miracles can take place.

~ Gardening ~

When you plant something, positively focus on the vision of it achieving its divine blueprint. Then the elementals will help this to happen.

~ Education ~

Education means to draw out. We are asked not to impose our information on others for that is not education. Rather listen to the person you are educating, bring forward their wisdom and encourage them to develop their talents, using praise as a tool. The person you are teaching will open up like a flower to give and receive.

~ Work and business ~

Be true to your highest integrity. Truth has a vibration that others sense and it makes them feel safe for they know they can trust you. Then you will automatically attract work that is right for you. This applies whether you are employed or in charge of a business.

~ Self care ~

When you treat yourself with love, honour and respect, it has a magical alchemical effect on your body and your life. Every cell records the positive energy you are sending to yourself. It impacts on your DNA and changes even deeply entrenched genetic patterns. It keeps you happy and healthy and attracts like-minded, high-frequency people into your life. Your positivity helps you flow towards your destiny.

When you hold the purest intention, are true to yourself and are positive, your life is always joyous.

~ Relationships ~

Positively envisage a loving balance of giving and receiving within your relationships and they will transform in a miraculous way.

~ Food and drink ~

Good, pure food and water nourish our cells, keep our bodies healthy and our minds in balance. When you bless food and water, the angelic energy helps to keep your frequency high if you appreciate it and give thanks for it.

~ The Media ~

Regardless of what you see or read you must intuit if it feels right and make up your own mind.

The media spreads information. Where this is inspirational and informative it can raise the frequency of millions of people.

If the media is reporting news of a disaster, it gives the world an opportunity to send compassion and healing to raise the vibration.

The alchemy is that together we can transform, transmute, inspire and enlighten each other as well as situations. The magic is that it brings us all together as one.

~ Creativity ~

Creativity unlocks divine expression, sacred geometry, beauty, alchemy and magic within us. A painting, a building or a garden can inspire and raise our frequency. Such inspired creativity is magic in that it opens us to God.

■ **The KEY is that when you express the truth of your soul, magic occurs.**

■ **The SOUND is the clear note of truth.**

■ **The COLOUR is crystal clear.**

EXERCISE: *To treat yourself with respect*

1. Make a chart for one week to record:
2. What food are you eating? Is it nourishing and good for you?
3. What exercise are you taking? Walking, yoga, the gym, swimming?
4. How are you cleansing your body and your face?
5. How are you relaxing?
6. How much leisure time have you programmed into your week?
7. How have you responded to people? Are you choosing a laughter response?
8. Are you spending time in nature?

Take time to allow more of what you need into your life.

EXERCISE: *Visualization to create alchemy and magic*

1. Find a place where you can be quiet and undisturbed.
2. Light a candle if possible.
3. Relax and close your eyes.
4. Ground yourself by imagining roots going from you deep into the earth.
5. Place Archangel Michael's blue cloak of protection around you.
6. Imagine something that you would really love to create or do. It can be anything from painting a picture, creating a garden to being a politician.
7. Sit quietly and feel the truth or essence of this.
8. In your inner world create your vision.
9. See yourself talking to others about it and hear the ring of truth as you speak.
10. Where you one hundred percent, wholeheartedly feel this to be your truth, alchemy and magic will occur.
11. Open yourself up to be it.

Oneness

We are all one. All are aspects of Source and when you know this your frequency rises to that of Source. You see the light of God within everyone and, as you see it, you energize it to expand.

When you are in Oneness your heart is totally open. Your Illumined Self gives freely, receives gratefully, is utterly compassionate and empathetic. You accept everyone exactly as they are with glowing love in your heart. You are the heartbeat of the universe.

When you know Oneness you are open and clear about everything in the universe. You see and understand with gratitude the work of the elementals. You honour and love the angels. You walk hand in hand with the masters.

You communicate telepathically with rocks, crystals, plants, trees, elementals, the elements, animals, insects, people, angels, unicorns, masters, ancient wise ones and God.

You automatically bring forward your own ancient knowledge from this planet and your stellar connections. You can also telepathically access information, knowledge and wisdom from all sentient beings.

You live in the vibration of Truth, so you trust completely and feel safe. This automatically allows you to feel divine peace. You become claircogniscient, so you know all there is to know.

You are completely self-contained and in total balance. You are equally connected to the Earth and Heavens with a true sense of who you are as an Earth being.

You trust the divine flow and know all is provided. Under the Law of Attraction you draw in like souls and all radiate joy.

Your cells visibly radiate and glow.

Your intuitive understanding of sacred geometry means you are automatically aligned to the divine blueprint. You use it spontaneously at all times, for example when laying out food on your plate.

The qualities of the elements are balanced in your personality.

You know everything and are free. At the same time you rejoice in the daily wonder of life, the miracle of nature unfolding. You are pure and innocent.

Your twelve chakras are open at all times and you are fully connected with your soul, Monad, Source and Hollow Earth.

Kathy's angels said to her, 'The most amazing quality you can have is to accept who you are. Recognize how wonderful you are; know this at the deepest cell level; feel this energy shining strongly from you, through your aura and out into the universe, the other realms of existence and touching everything along the way. Appreciate how exhilarating this is for those who sense this, know how it is for you when you receive it, when others are glowing. Never ever underestimate the power of you. We have shared with you a snippet of the energy in the universe and have given you the Keys – the intention, the vision of colours and the sense of sounds for you to enjoy and to allow these to enfold you and support you on your journey of enlightenment and ascension. This is just the beginning. We love you all... your angelic friends.'

No one who has ever incarnated has yet attained Oneness but this information has been given to us because it is going to be possible to do so by 2032.

■ **The KEY is to know you are God.**

■ **The SOUND is every sound.**

■ **The COLOUR is black and white, yin and yang.**

EXERCISE: *Visualization to connect with your own divinity*

1. Find a place where you can be quiet and undisturbed.
2. Light a candle if possible.
3. Relax and close your eyes.
4. Ground yourself by imagining roots going from your feet deep into the earth.
5. Place Archangel Michael's blue cloak of protection around you.
6. See the great Universal Angel Metatron in front of you.
7. He is holding a mirror up in front of you in which you can see your inner beauty, your glory, your magnificence and your divine self.

8. As you see your true light feel your oneness with All That Is.
9 Relax into this knowing.
10. When you feel complete, return your awareness to the room and open your eyes.

EXERCISE: *To connect with Oneness*

- Consciously practise oneness today by practising what we share in this chapter.
- For example, open your heart to someone who has committed terrible atrocities and send him or her glowing love.
- Lay out your food according to sacred geometry.

Conclusion

We feel very privileged to have been given the information for this book and have endeavoured to keep our energy high in order to receive it in as pure a way as possible from Kumeka and the angels.

Through this work we have learned a tremendous amount and feel we have specific actions we can do and visualizations or exercises to help us attune directly to the Keys that open the doors to the secrets of the Universe.

We are watching and listening to everything that is presented to us in a totally new way as we start to access the wisdom of the ancients. It fills us with a sense of excitement as well as awe. We feel life will never be the same again.

~ Creating the CD ~

Kumeka informed us right from the start that we would need a CD with the book, containing all the sound keys for the universe. One section of this CD is for Hollow Earth and the other one for Sirius. Finally the sounds are incorporated like an orchestra. You may be able to pick out certain notes and keys but the aim is to listen to them together in harmony so that you are presented with all the Keys to the universe simultaneously. Then you can access them and use them once more to unlock the secrets known by the Wise Ancients. Through this, you will be one of those who hold the planet and all on her in the fifth dimension, so that all beings can ascend.

We had a most exciting, interesting and laughter-filled evening creating the sounds of the Keys. Kathy and I went to the home of a friend, Diane Egby-Edwards, who is a Master of Sound. She created all of the sounds, though some we added our voices to.

Kathy and I focussed the intention into each Key and by the end of the four-hour session my third eye was on fire! It really felt powerful and brought home to me the importance of the opportunities offered by the Keys. The sounds were recorded by Kit Gibbons; we had never met him before, but he intuitively understood what we needed and was clearly sent by the angels. We were absolutely thrilled when we heard the completed CD he created.

~ The Sound Keys on CD ~

The attached CD contains the sound keys for the universe. Please activate these keys by listening to them, so that you, the whole world and this universe will benefit: the Keys are that important. When you listen to the sound keys with your heart open, you will start your attunement to the Cosmic Keys held in Hollow Earth and Sirius.

The CD is divided into three sections:

- Unique sounds for the Keys 1 – 48
- The cosmic orchestra for Hollow Earth
- The cosmic orchestra for Sirius

After you have read a key it is suggested that you listen to the sound for that key, so that the angels can align you to the frequency. As you listen to the Hollow Earth and Sirius cosmic orchestras you may be able to pick out certain notes and keys but the aim is to listen to them together in harmony, so that you are presented with all the Keys to the universe. You can then access them and use them once more to unlock the secrets known by the Wise Ancients. With this you will be one of those who hold the planet and all on her in the fifth dimension, so that ascension can be achieved.

We hope you enjoy the sounds like we did when we were given them.

We give thanks to Diane Egby-Edwards for her amazing musical skills, to Kit Gibbons for the orchestration and production of the CD, and to Mike Koenig for the use of some of his recorded sounds.

Diane Egby-Edwards – www.degby.wetpaint.com
Kit Gibbons – www.gibbonda.com
Mike Koenig – www.soundbible.com

~ Summary of the Keys to the Universe ~

	Key	Sound	Colour	Held by/at
48 Connected Keys				
1	Relax deeply and honour the animals and the Earth	the clarion call inviting everyone to live in the fifth dimension	gold	Atlantis
2	Connect to Source and bring your energy into balance with the true unconditional love of the Earth	the low hum connecting the four ascension planets	white-gold	Lemuria
3	Bring together the wisdom of all the planets	wind singing through the trees, music in the hills	pale yellow	Mu
4	Reconnect with the ancient knowledge, wisdom and light held within the core of Africa Fuse with the energy of the Elemental Masters	drumming like the heartbeat of the planet	purple green	Petranium
5	Completely trust Source that you can create something unique and wonderful	the sound of birth, the heartbeat	pure white	Angala
6	Feel your feet in the Earth and love in your heart while listening to the sound of the didgeridoo	the didgeridoo	green	The Aborigines
7	Understand the use of energy to bring everything into harmony, alignment and wholeness	a whoop of joy from the heart and humming from the heart	gold	The Incas

8	Understand and love who you truly are, so that you are in tune with your divine blueprint and the planet	silence followed by a gentle ting on cymbals	pink gold	The Aztecs
9	Work with what nature provides for the greater good and understand and apply the spiritual laws	the sound of running water	crystal with green aquamarine	The Babylonians
10	Connect to the six-pointed star and thus bring Earth to Heaven and Heaven to Earth	a high-frequency, high-pitched sound, like a grasshopper and the gentle whoosh of angel wings	royal blue	The Egyptians
11	Remain pure and connected to your guidance	the sound of water dripping from an icicle	blue-white of pure ice	The Innuits
12	Honour the land and all things living on and within it	the fast drum of the heartbeat of the land	red and brown	The Native Americans
13	Attune to the wisdom of the dolphins Explore Earth and the far reaches of the universe	the sound of the conch shell	silver blue	The Kahunas of Hawaii
14	Live in compassion, harmlessness and peace and enter the Silence	chanting	white	The Tibetans
15	Hold love in your heart and breathe it out to nature, so that the world continues to grow and blossom	tinkling laughter and tinkling bells; the flute	pink	The Mayans
16	Bring everything in the cosmos into resonance and harmony	the sound of stars singing and plants growing	green gold	The Mesopotamians

17	Develop the mind, so that it can heal the body	the harp connecting everything in the universe	mid-yellow	The Greek culture
18	Develop intuition and attune to the sacred mysteries of the universe	clapping	mid-blue	The Maoris
19.	Connect to the figure of eight	the humming of the pyramid connecting to the universe	crimson red	Great Pyramid and Sphinx, Egypt
20	Heal from the heart by enfolding all in love	angels singing	blue-white	Mount Shasta, California
21	Spread and focus unconditional love	the hum from the heart that connects the crystal skull, stars and sacred geometry	pale crystal pink	Mayan Cosmic Pyramid, Guatemala
22	Balance the masculine and feminine energy to bring about harmonious co-existence	a low soft gong rippling out into silence	Pleiadean blue	Gobi Desert, Asia
23	Understand and follow the spiritual law	a gong getting louder	shimmering pearl	Cosmic Pyramid, Greece
24	Relax totally into deep, divine, inner peace, the peace that passeth all understanding	the sound of the wings of a dove	brilliant white	Great Cosmic Pyramid, Tibet
25	Trust your intuition and use it wisely and strongly for the highest good	the shriek of the condor	silver moonstone	Pyramid under Machu Picchu, Peru
26	Have inner peace and follow the divine will	innocent laughter	rainbow	Hollow Earth portal, USA
27	Develop and practise agape or higher love	angels singing about love	rose pink	Honolulu
28	Bring in the wisdom of Sirius through sacred geometry	the sound of dancing bare feet on soft earth	royal blue	Dogon Portal, Mali, Africa

29	Tune into the Great Crystal of Atlantis with expectation	the murmur of a rippling sea	sea-green	Bermuda Triangle
30	Practise friendship, warmth, together-ness and co-oper-ation to promote harmony at a fifth-dimensional level	the sound of celebration	orange	Ocean near Fiji
31	Take in the qualities that the birds teach us through the vibration of the sound they make	the singing of the dawn chorus	azure blue of a clear sky	Bird Kingdom
32	Honour, respect and embrace the animal kingdom	the chatter of monkeys	gold yellow through to white	Animal Kingdom
33	Drink, bathe in and bless pure water; open yourself to the wisdom of the water kingdom	whales and dolphins calling	aquamarine	Kingdom of ocean beings
34	Acknowledge the importance of the elemental kingdom	high-pitched melodious humming	green	Elemental Kingdom
35	Ask for help for the highest good	an orchestra of harps	gold	Angelic Kingdom
36	Discover your original divine blueprint	sounds of the qualities taken up on the breath to a higher level	gold	Deva & Reptile Kingdom
37	Let go and go with the flow	Silence	crystal clear	Time and speed
38	Live your truth	one tap on a crystal bowl	transparent white	Other dimensions
39	Know that you are linked to all the stars, planets and galaxies	hum of the divine cosmic flow	silver and gold entwined	Other planets, stars and galaxies

40	Connect with earth, air, fire and water and bring the qualities they carry into perfect balance	silence and stillness	white	Nature Kingdom (Elements)
	Air – attune to the air elementals and breathe in their higher traits			
	Fire – light a candle, connect to Nigellay, Mars, and draw in the fire qualities			
	Water – relax in water, connect to Neptune and call in the water qualities			
	Earth – go into nature, link to Hollow Earth through your Earth Star chakra and draw in the earth qualities			
41	Understand and trust the divine in all things	water lapping	orange	Sacred Geometry
42	Consciously expand your aura at all times	a cosmic harmony	White-blue	Light
43	Do everything with the purest intention	angels singing	pale yellow gold	Sonic sounds
44	Treat yourself and others as a perfect divine being	an angelic harp	black and white, the yin and yang symbol	Qualities for Golden Earth
45	Ask the angels to conduct your spirit in your sleep to the cosmic heart and enfold your spirit there	the sound of a baby receiving love	gold, white and pink	Cosmic heart

46	Be in the moment to receive a flow of angelic love	the heart beating	aquamarine (receiving)	Pure love – divine connection
	Give from the heart and the angels will add their energy		rose pink (giving)	
47	Express the truth of your soul and magic occurs	the clear note of truth	crystal clear	Spiritual Laws
48	Know you are God	every sound	black and white, yin and yang	Oneness

	Key	Sound	Colour	Held by/at
2 Golden Cosmic Keys				
49	Tune into the blueprint of the planet	the cosmic orchestra of all the sounds	azure blue	Hollow Earth
50	Understand the Universal Metatron Cube	the cosmic orchestra of all the sounds	blue green	Sirius

The Diana Cooper School, a not for profit organization, runs teacher training courses throughout the world in Angels, Ascension, Atlantis, Transform Your Life, 2012 and Beyond as well as Lemurian healing. See www.dianacooperschool.com.

FINDHORN PRESS

Life Changing Books

For a complete catalogue,
please contact:

Findhorn Press Ltd
117-121 High Street,
Forres IV36 1AB,
Scotland, UK

t +44 (0)1309 690582
f +44 (0)131 777 2711
e info@findhornpress.com

or consult our catalogue online
(with secure order facility) on
www.findhornpress.com

For information on the Findhorn Foundation:
www.findhorn.org